HOW I FACED MY FEARS

*A spiritual journey
to turning challenges
into success*

VERENA MARTIN

Copyright © 2020 Verena Martin

All rights reserved.

No part of this book may be reproduced in any manner, mechanically or electronically, including tape or other audio recordings and photocopying, without the written permission of the author, except for reasonable excerpts for research and reviewing purposes.

ISBN: 978-1-77605-671-2

First published in 2019 under the title 'Why Fear is your Friend'
ISBN: 978-1-77605-608-8 (Printed version)
ISBN: 978-1-77605-607-1 (e-book)

Published by Kwarts Publishers
www.kwartspublishers.co.za

Contact the author:
E-mail: verena@verenamartin.online
Website: verenamartin.online

HOW TO USE FEAR AS
YOUR OWN POWER SOURCE
AND LIVE THE LIFE
YOU WANT TO

VERENA MARTIN

CONTENTS

PREFACE 7

1	Stand Up for Yourself	11
2	Have Faith	21
3	Start	29
4	Never Give Up	37
5	Facing Your Fears	43
6	Take Full Responsibility for Your Life	51
7	Ask the Universe	57
8	Trust Your Intuition	65
9	Find Peace in Being Alone	73
10	Tomorrow Is Another Day	81
11	Set Goals	87
12	Make a Plan	97
13	Don't Wait	103
14	Keep Moving	111
15	Be Thankful	121
16	Have Respect	129

PREFACE

When I was 7 years old, I remember swinging happily in our garden when I heard a loud roar in the sky. It startled me so that I had to look up and investigate it. As I gazed at the sky I immediately saw that it was an airplane and it left such an interesting, white and puffy strip behind it. All of the sudden a yearning emerged from deep within me, so strongly that I'll never forget it. Yes, I wanted to be on that plane, free to roam and explore the world even at such a young age. It was a pivotal experience for me because at that exact moment I became determined to follow my dreams and create the very best life for myself.

Of course, I didn't know that I had such a long and sometimes challenging journey ahead of me. After all, I was viewing the world through a child's perspective. Today I know better. I understand that we are all on journeys that often swerve, twist and turn – that's one of the many things we all share in common. I also know that it's not so much the target of the journey that's so delightful. It's the journey – the way – itself that makes living so wonderful.

Life is a playing field where we can test and prove ourselves as a means of growing and developing as the unique individuals that we truly are. Everything is about experiences. We need to learn from them and get better at living as we move on toward our dreams each day. When we're young and our egos are strong, we tend to struggle easily and become discouraged when we fall or fail. It's extremely difficult to pick ourselves up by the bootstraps, stand up again and leave the failures behind us. However, when we get older we begin to realize that everyone fails at one time or another and that makes life a lot easier to bear. It's part of being a human being. That's why it's so very important to tell our stories to each other, so that others can become inspired and motivated for their own life's journey.

The purpose of this book is to share much of my life's story with you as a means of illustrating how I've come up with 16 ways to living a better and happier life. I put a lot of thought into this because I'm not a fan of so many of the articles and books that say they can show you "5 Habits that Can Lead to Happiness!" It's not so much what the habits are that concerns me. They're usually pretty sound suggestions. It's the lack of preparation provided to the reader in order for he or she to benefit from them that troubles me. There are many good coaches and DVDs out there but I also hear from so many people that they didn't work for them. They're still not on a safe journey and don't feel secure. They may feel okay today but when something difficult happens tomorrow, they stumble. Again, I believe the main culprit is that these people have not been taught to do the ground work first. It's like sowing seed on bad soil. Nothing takes.

So what kind of preparation is required? It's been my experience that we all need to be totally aware and connected to ourselves before we can even begin to benefit from anything we are taught. We have to know our weaknesses, our strengths, our fears. This frightens many people I speak with but it shouldn't because once you know what makes you tick you'll be confident enough to face those weakness and fears. You'll also learn how to grow your strengths and be open to new lessons and suggestions. You just can't do it blindly.

We seem to focus our attention on everything outside of us and very rarely look deep inside. We really can't be blamed for it because we've been conditioned to do so by our society – now more than ever. We need to close the gap, be aware and take responsibility for our own universe. Then we can think about working with coaches and self-help books successfully.

That's why I wrote this book. I want you to have the tools necessary to be safe on your life's journey, feeling secure no matter what turns up on your path. My hope is that after reading these pages, you'll let the waves come and go but you'll stay the same – stable like a mountain, letting the storms pass you by and never rock you to the core. Of course, you'll be affected by the unexpected detours in your journey, but they'll never make you insecure in your universe because you are whole. Your roots will be planted firmly in the ground and you'll be flexible like a palm tree that sways in the wind but never falls.

What's more, you'll learn to see each event in your life – difficult or joyous – as a gift. That will all happen when you change your focus to inside and oh, what wonderful things you'll discover there. You'll also learn that you're not on your journey alone. We're all sitting in the same boat and we are one. Isn't that magical? I think so, and I know you will, too!

1

STAND UP FOR YOURSELF

I GREW UP IN A QUITE WEALTHY, entrepreneurial family in Germany where tradition and religion determined everything in our lives. My father tragically lost his first wife after a kidney operation when she was only 33 years old and was left a widower to raise 3 little children. It may seem a little strange by today's standards, but my Mom was one of 3 women who were selected to be his next wife. So, Dad left the decision to his children. After all, he thought, they were the best candidates to select the woman who would be caring for them while he was at work and traveling. So, the kids voted for my Mom. Quite a democracy!

Dad and Mom were married in January and I was born in October. They didn't believe in wasting any time. For them I was their only child. However, I was always very aware of the fact that I was the only one who was not a member of the previous family. My half-sisters and half-brother were also many years older than I was. I therefore felt lonely, different and mostly lost as a child. So, I tried to compensate by being everybody's little darling for many years until I realized that it didn't help me feel more connected to the family. In fact, it only disconnected me from myself.

It also didn't help that my parents' marriage was like a rollercoaster – passion, tears, escalations, addictions and harmony all rolled up into one relationship. It was like living in a Hollywood production – and not particularly entertaining to watch. They couldn't be together, but they also couldn't live apart. After a while, my mother began to drink too much and my father grew more and more upset. At times things elevated to ugly proportions, but they always managed to get through it and move on together. They were in many ways heroes for me because they were authentic in the way they lived, always true to themselves – both their good and sometimes dark sides.

That being said, I remember one fight that was particularly horrible when I was 16 years old. It culminated with my Mom falling down the stairs of our villa. I immediately ran to her side and saw that blood was gushing out of her head. I was horrified. Believe me, I didn't view my father as a hero that night. When the emergency workers carried Mom out the front door to the ambulance, my Dad stood calmly at that door. I began to follow them when he stopped me and said, "If you go with her to the hospital, you won't be able to step foot into this house ever again." I told the emergency workers to wait for me, ran up to my room and grabbed some money, the keys for my bike and a warm jacket. I then came back down, looked at my Dad squarely in the eyes and told him "Goodbye." I walked out of the house, shut the door behind me and mounted my bike to follow Mom to the hospital.

At that point, I was 100% certain that I would need to make a plan for myself. I had to find a place to live and figure out how I would finish my schooling. The first night Mom was in the hospital, I stayed at my brother's house. The next day I asked my girlfriend if I could stay a week with her and her parents allowed it. I was set for a week, at least.

On Sunday evening I called our housekeeper and asked if she would ask my Dad if I could come over to pack some clothes and school stuff. She inquired on my behalf and said he would allow it. When I arrived, Dad asked me if we could speak. I really didn't want to but felt I owed it to him. After all, he was still my father. He led me to his bedroom and closed the door behind us. To my surprise, he began to cry and fell to his knees, apologizing. I was stunned.

This truly was a gift. Dad was such a strong and seemingly perfect man. I really respected him and yes, was afraid of him at times. Nevertheless, I loved him very much. It was the first time he revealed his true feelings to me, and the very first time I stood up to him. In fact, it was the very first time I stood up for myself period. This incident changed our whole relationship for the better, and forever.

I believe this story is a great example of how standing up for yourself can lead to wonderful results. Most of the time, people don't really know what's going on inside of you. Your outward behavior, in most cases, doesn't reveal what you are truly thinking and feeling. The only way to connect to people, situations and life itself is by standing up for yourself and revealing your feelings. We often feel that we'll hurt someone or be rude if we do, but that's not true at all. Just calmly explain what you're thinking about a circumstance and what you're really feeling deep inside you – but always in an honest and respectful way. Don't be shy. You're a valuable part of the universe. Bring to light what's inside of you – make it visible. When you do that the energy will be clear and I promise you that everything can be solved. Your relationships can even become stronger and deeper.

* * *

As we'll see in a later chapter, standing up for ourselves always involves taking 100% responsibility for of all our actions and decisions. On a subconscious level we always think that someone will rescue us – parents, husbands, friends, etc. However, when we change our focus from the outside to the inside and take responsibility, we're set free and that gives us energy and power. We're not waiting until something or someone comes to whisk us away and save us. We're not victims. We have everything we need inside to stand up for ourselves with conviction. We are magical. The only problem is that we forgot it. We came here as souls and actually chose beforehand where we were to be born, what our bodies would look like and what our weaknesses and strengths would be. Our souls want to be on this journey that we chose for ourselves. Take it and trust and believe that you are able to make the journey and enjoy it.

At this point, you might be saying, "Verena, how can I do this – it's easier said than done?" I understand how you might feel that way, but it's actually not as difficult as it seems. You first need to look at your values, which actually define you and are your structure. Begin by making a list of your core values, and place them in order of priority. The categories usually include your personal life, your career and your social life. Subcategories might include God, children, husband, health, money, fame, position, nightlife, adventure, travel, etc. You'll know what your values are when you sit and concentrate on what makes you happiest in life.

Then choose 3 top values that you would take with you if you needed to make a decision. After that, start living with these values as your base. For some people their top value is loyalty or spirituality. For others it might be faith or honesty. Do you put career first? Does your family take precedence over everything? Or do you place your friendships above everything else? Don't be concerned about people who judge your value system. It's your life and only you need to believe in what your value structure is and what makes you tick. When you begin to live on the basis of your core values, I guarantee you that you'll never feel disconnected from yourself. It will also make it much easier for you to take responsibility and make important decisions.

For instance, if your family is more important to you than your career, then you need to own that and never waiver, no matter what. So, if your boss asks you to stay later one evening but you need to be at your child's recital, you can confidently say "I can't because my child needs me for support tonight." You'll do it without the fear of losing your job because you'll be in harmony with yourself and things will come together because you are living authentically. Your life will be balanced. In addition, your boss will most likely respect that you are living your life according to your values and priorities. If not, then you shouldn't be working for him or her anyway because if you have different values, then other problems will arise as well. What's important is you stood up for yourself based on your values. Just move on to a better job!

* * *

My journey to being able to stand up for myself came with lots of learning experiences. By nature, I'm a fearful person and always want to be in harmony with everything and everyone. You could imagine what a challenge standing up for myself was at times. As I said, I always wanted to be everyone's darling but that didn't work out for me. It only made the people around me want to make decisions for me – especially my father and ex-husband. However, I found that when people took care of me it only served to pull me down. It turns out that my soul wants to be independent and strong.

This was apparent at the very beginning of my life. When I was a baby, my father hired a nanny to take care of me. After all, my mother was young and there were already 3 children from his first marriage with which to deal. After a while under the nanny's care, he became concerned because I never cried. He had experience with children and was used to babies crying all the time. It turned out that the nanny was giving me chemicals in very high dosages to keep me calm. I guess one time she forgot to administer the medication because I started to cry so loud that I gave myself a hernia. It was as if I were screaming out, "Hey world, I'm here!" When I had the hernia surgery at six months, it was discovered that I was being drugged. Of course, the nanny was fired.

This is typical in my life's story. When someone tries to keep me quiet – you know, shut up and be pretty – I don't take it. As difficult as it was at times, I learned to stand up for myself and never give up. It was my destiny to be in these kinds of situations and I've had to constantly fight them. The fact is, I never felt comfortable with people taking care of me and not letting me go my own way. I don't want to be supported. I want to support myself.

For instance, when I was married to my ex-husband, all he was interested in was having me look good, accompany him to social functions, and then go back to our villa until he was ready to show me off again. I wasn't happy with that kind of life but didn't dare think about divorce because I was Catholic.

When my daughter Lara was born, she brought happiness back into my life. I made her my first priority and was doing all right for a while. However, just before she started to walk I became very ill with constant diarrhea for 6 months. I went to many doctors but no one could tell me what was wrong. I was afraid to eat and lost too much weight. Of course, I always thought twice about stepping out of the house for fear of becoming sick. I was turning into a recluse.

Our nanny – a lovely woman from Barbados – became very concerned about me. She suggested that I visit with her friend who read tarot cards. I was against the idea because at the time I thought it involved black magic or something. However, I was getting sicker and sicker so I decided to visit the reader anyway. She used medical tarot cards and the first time she laid them on the table 9 diarrhea cards were revealed! Realizing there was something to this, I decided to become more proactive and my research brought me to an excellent clinic in Hamburg.

After a full examination and many tests, the doctor scheduled me for a colonoscopy and biopsy. He said if he didn't find something, I would still have a problem. If he did discover something wrong, he would give me 6 months to live because I was young and the illness would most certainly be aggressive. After the procedure, when I woke up in the recovery room, I began to cry because I instinctively knew I was healthy. I even told the doctor that he didn't have to send me the results because I knew I was okay.

When I went home, I said to myself, "This is the first day of my life." I began to do daily affirmations. I would write, "I am strong...I am healthy...I am loveable...I can take care of myself." After 6 weeks I began to focus on my strengths and told my husband that I was giving our marriage 365 days to change for the better. He didn't take me seriously, typically, and nothing changed. So, after a year I left. That's the day that my daughter Lara walked for the very first time – her first step towards her own independence!

As you can see, my whole life was about fighting authority. My father never discussed anything, he just did it. Once I bought a car he didn't like, so he just declared that I was going to sell it. Back then he had the power to make me feel that I couldn't stand up for myself and fight him.

That day my mother was sent to the hospital was the first day I stood up for myself, and it brought great results. The second time I did it was when I left my husband. I learned to stand up and take control of my life. Believe me, it wasn't easy but most worthy things in life don't come easily. However, it becomes more effortless with practice. It's made me stronger, and most important, happy.

I also want to stress that standing up for myself has never hurt any relationship that was worth having to begin with. To this day, I have a good relationship with my ex-husband. We share a wonderful gift – Lara – and enjoy her together. As for my father, we continued to have our ups and downs but loved each other dearly until the day he died. My soul chose to be on a journey with him, and still does. Your soul always chooses the same path every time it incarnates – it's just the circumstances that change. In a past life, I was my father's son and he exiled me out of his kingdom because I rebelled. When we came back in this life, he made reforms. You choose your souls and they're here for a reason. My husband is a fairly young soul and he always wants to be with me in each life. I choose him as well.

* * *

In summary, standing up for yourself involves knowing what you want. Knowing what you truly desire comes by recognizing your values and prioritizing them. Devote enough time into being absolutely clear about what your personal values are in the different facets of your life. It's crucial because it prepares your whole life's plan and defines the very meaning of your existence. When you do this and are committed to setting these priorities and living in line with them – no matter what – you'll enrich your life and be a balanced, mature person in society. You'll immediately feel more connected to yourself and gain inner strength. You'll also sleep better and feel more relaxed, calm and satisfied.

You are in charge so take back control and use that awesome power to create your own life and set your own goals. Stand up for yourself and never, ever allow people or situations to change your personal priorities. Don't let them distracted you or push you around, either. Always demand the respect you deserve. Set boundaries and let everyone know what works for you and what doesn't. That strength will attract the people who suit you best and everything in your life will fall into place.

2

HAVE FAITH

WHEN I LOOK AT WHAT'S GOING ON in someone else's life, I always know there is a deeper meaning behind it. As long as I can stand outside myself and observe the circumstances of my own life – as if I were another person – I can also see that there is profound significance behind the pendulum of my journey. It's all about having faith. We need to have this faith because there is always something moving underneath the events and circumstances of our lives – experiences that are much bigger than first meets the eye. The truth is, our minds are much too small to get it. When you travel in a hypnotic state, however, you can almost always see it clearly.

Of course, we can't all walk around in a hypnotic state. However, we can have faith that things are happening for a reason because we have the support of the universe. Naturally, we all have choices. Our lives are our own and indeed are not written in stone. Nevertheless, we all need to look to the universe for signs to help us understand why something is happening. Just as important, the universe will guide us to make the right decisions and walk the path we were meant to follow.

It's funny, when something good happens to us we never ask why. We just assume that it's because of the work we've put in, or perhaps just plain old good luck. What about the sadder events in our lives? Perhaps we experience the death of a parent, or we lose a job or get divorced. Whatever the case, many of us then tend lose faith. We resist and mourn and don't follow the course that the universe is setting before us. We're lost and sometimes even die because the soul is not in sync with the direction it chose to follow before we got here. It therefore has to come back to find the right direction and follow the course.

The fact is, if you lose something and it's gone forever, that's because it should be that way. Open up to see the signs that the universe is confirming for you. Here's a nice story I'd like to share with you. There is a young soul who always wanted to go to earth. She looks down on our planet and its inhabitants and feels it's all so wonderous. When she asks God if he would send her to earth, he tells her she doesn't know what she's asking. She'd better stay where she is and enjoy the peace and serenity of that celestial existence. However, she insists that she wants to experience life on earth.

God sees he's not going to convince her otherwise, so he asks what experiences she'd like to have on earth. She tells him that she desires to be hurt badly by someone she loves and then learn what it's like to forgive. God realizes what a challenge that would be for her, so he calls an older soul in for a consultation. When the young soul tells the older soul what she wants, the older soul explains that she doesn't realize how difficult that would be for her. Nevertheless, the young soul insists.

God and the old soul give in and call another old soul to accompany her on her journey. Before they leave, the old companion soul tells her, "I'm going to give you the most difficult time imaginable. No matter what, though, I don't ever want you to forget who I really am and why I'm accompanying you on your journey."

So, you see, when someone does something really bad to you, have faith that it all has a deeper reason. It's always a gift. Your soul chose to experience what it is to cry, to love and lose, to kiss and hug, or to have pain. It just needed to be in your body to accomplish it. It also needed to have the souls it chose to walk with you on your particular journey. They all have a reason for being with you. It bears repeating: You chose this journey and the people in your life, even if you don't realize it. This is a critical point that we all must understand. If you're not willing to go with it – to have faith that it's all happening because it's supposed to occur – then you'll constantly be wrestling and struggling. In fact, you'll have to leave this life and come back until you get it right.

* * *

Although having faith isn't always easy, there are some practical tips to achieving it. For instance, if you have a problem that's too big for you, walk away from it and give it up to your higher subconscious. Leave it for another time and another day. We'll talk more about this later on, but for now believe me when I say that signs with a solution will definitely come to you. Soon a book with the answer will suddenly fall from a bookshelf in your home office. Or you'll stumble upon a blog that will inspire you with a resolution. It will come. The key is not to fight your circumstance but to try to walk with it all and have faith that there is a higher plan. Lost your job? Don't fight or cry. Know – have faith – that something better will come along because it surely will. Difficulties are gifts. I promise you.

This may sound silly at first, but if you physically keep bumping into things the universe may very well be sending you a sign. It's probably telling you, "Stop! You need to take some time to think about what's happening in your life!" At that point, give some serious thought to what's out of balance in your life. You probably already know what it is but don't want to face it because it involves change, and almost everyone is uncomfortable with change. That's mostly because they feel that they have to face something out of their comfort zone alone. Don't panic. Have faith that the universe knows what it's doing and trust in this bigger plan that change will help bring about. Take the chance and receive the gifts that this time of challenge is offering you, courtesy of the universe.

It also helps to remember that you cannot experience good if you've never experienced bad. You wouldn't be able to recognize it because you would have nothing with which to compare it. Life is never all day. There has to be night as well. To experience love, you have to experience hate. That's the law of dualism in life.

I know another story that can help guide you on your way to having faith. A man and Jesus were silently walking along a sandy beach together, both leaving a set of footprints in the sand. As the man looked to the sky, he began to see scenes of his life flash before his eyes. When the last scene was over, the man looked back and noticed that during the happiest times of his life, there were two sets of footprints. However, during the most difficult moments, there was only one set of footprints. The man asked Jesus why he left him alone during those sad times. Jesus told him that he only sees one set of footprints because it was during those hard times that he carried him. You see, we're never alone and you never get more than you can carry when you have faith.

* * *

Some people hear the word "faith" and immediately associate it with institutional religion, in which they've been highly disappointed. They therefore feel they aren't into the idea of faith and never will be. They should realize that belief systems and faith were implanted into our subconscious during our childhood. Even if unhappy experiences within the religions they were raised weakened their faith and filled them with doubts, everyone is able to change and learn to have faith again. I urge those who feel this way to consider that having faith is like possessing an invisible connection to ourselves and our creator, whoever that may be for them. Then they'll know that there is something bigger supporting them and that will give them inner peace.

In my belief system, faith has nothing to do with religion. I actually believe in everything – Hinduism, Buddhism, Christianity, Judaism, etc. – because all of these religions give us a possible framework with which to have faith. However, they are structure and symbolism, not faith itself. You can choose to be Catholic, or just believe in the universe, but you must have faith. Only then will you see how, as this magical life enfolds in so many fascinating ways, you can observe with wonder and connect with the magnificence of a bigger plan that exists for all of us.

* * *

As with everything, it takes learning experiences to have faith. After I finished school I decided to study fashion design. Things were going really well and I enjoyed my student life and being creative. One day I went to my gynecologist for a checkup. After the exam, she told me that there was a tumor in my uterus the size of a tennis ball. The following weeks were devastating for me. I had to take chemo medication and lost lots of my hair. I thought the world was coming to an end.

The chemo hadn't worked so the doctor said I needed to enter the hospital immediately and have the tumor removed. I wanted to postpone the surgery until after the weekend so I could be at my Dad's 60th birthday celebration in the south of Germany. The doctor advised me not to wait, but of course, being so young I thought I was invincible and postponed it anyway.

When I returned I entered the hospital, frightened to death. Before my surgery, the doctor came to visit me with a young, really handsome doctor accompanying him. I was so smitten with him that I called my girlfriend and asked her to immediately bring my blow dryer and hair straightener so I could look my best the next time the young doctor came to visit, which was to be in the afternoon.

Of course, this young doctor saw what I had done and realized what was going on. I was so embarrassed! It didn't matter though, because I was glad he saw me looking put together – not at my best, mind you – but at least presentable.

The tumor was removed successfully but I needed to stay in the hospital for 10 days. During that time the handsome doctor visited me many times and we got to know each other well. He asked me for a date when I was discharged and 4 weeks later we travelled together to Bali because he was half Indonesian and half German and wanted to introduce me to his father. Fast forward 3 years and we were married. This young, handsome doctor was my first husband!

You can say that anyone would think that having a tumor in her uterus is a bad thing. Why me? I'm going to die? Why does everything happen to me? That's what's visible on the surface. Of course, if having a tumor didn't happen to me I would never have met my first husband. That was the unseen reason for the tumor. It didn't kill me and I really enjoyed my time with my husband. If I had the faith then that I do now, I might still have been nervous but I would have totally believed that there was a reason for this seemingly unfortunate circumstance.

Have faith because underlying everything in our lives – monumental or small – is a greater design which we cannot see. When something challenges you, open your mind and face it with faith. You can be sure that there is something which you have to learn or change, or someone you need to meet. At the end of the day, something good will come from it. It's never about the cards that life deals us. Instead, it's all about how we react and work with those cards. Faith makes that a lot easier.

* * *

As you can see, there are many benefits to having faith. For one thing, you'll have more energy to face the challenges in your life. When these challenges arise, you'll face them head on and feel empowered and supported because you'll understand that there is a good reason for what seems bad, and you'll look forward to discovering what that good thing is.

Think of the inner confidence and peace you'll experience when you no longer perceive yourself as a powerless victim of bad luck. You'll become the creator and manager of your own life. People will pick up on that and will be more willing to be with you and even help you when you need it most. You'll be accustomed to saying "Yes" to life and to yourself.

Everyone is on his or her personal journey. Yes, life is often very challenging, but to be able to live fully you need to jump in and experience it. There is no other way to live. Having faith gives you this invisible lifebelt when you leap. You know it's there and if you have faith you'll feel the energy and the power. You'll possess the unwavering knowledge deep inside yourself that everything in your life will be fine. You'll become more confident, develop inner strength and have a deeper awareness of the infinite and magical existence of the universal mind.

3

START

WHEN MY DAD PASSED AWAY AFTER A very long illness, I decided to move to another country. As a kid, I always wanted to go somewhere different. (Remember that time I saw the airplane from my garden swing?) My siblings would always get homesick when we were away from home for any length of time. Not me. So, after the ordeal of my father's illness, I really needed a break – a new start, a new life. The perfect time to "go." I went with it and took my 5-year-old daughter on a trip to check out Cape Town, South Africa. I figured this would be a great place for us to live since they speak English and there's a huge German-speaking community there as well. Besides, Cape Town is quite modern and very European, so the culture shock for me and my daughter would be minimal.

I made an appointment at the German-English school and was overwhelmed by the warm welcome we received from the director and the students. Everyone there was amazing and my daughter loved the school. The director told me to relocate soon so that my daughter could start in the beginning of January, when the school year started. You see, school terms in South Africa are the opposite of those in Europe.

I then had an appointment with an immigration lawyer to check out the possibility of acquiring a long-term visa. I was relieved to hear that I was eligible, and that my dream was now becoming a reality. I then rented a temporary apartment close to the new school and booked a flight for the end of December. We were set up in Cape Town.

When we returned to Hamburg I had just 6 weeks to find a tenant for my apartment, sell all my furniture, pack the boxes for shipping and prepare the documents for our relocation. I did it all by myself and on top of that, Christmas was fast approaching. Of course, it's the most special time of the year for kids, so I wanted to be sure my daughter wasn't cheated out of all of the fun. I therefore made a list, shopped for her presents and stayed up till morning wrapping everything.

You may ask how I managed all of that. Well, I really didn't have any time to ponder what could go wrong. I didn't stop to think if I were making the right decision or even what our new life would look like. I turned myself into a sort of robot and just got started and kept going. In the end, everything went much better than I could have ever imagined. We lived in Cape Town for 5 years and I have to say it was probably one of the greatest, most valuable times in our lives.

* * *

We often need to remind ourselves to start. I don't know, maybe it's more of a female thing because men seem to be in a constant state of moving. Women seem to pose. Both men and women, though, think and discuss more than we need to. We try to analyze everything before we make a decision – the positives, the negatives, the what ifs. Then we become paralyzed. We don't realize that perhaps if we just do it, take the first step and see how it goes, that we can always make adjustments and have plenty of support along the way. I assure you, if I had overthought our move to Cape Town, I would have convinced myself that it was too much of leap and never would have gone. We then would have missed out on an experience of a lifetime.

The fact is, when we're facing opportunities in our lives, we often react to them as if they were challenges. However, acting upon opportunities is the only way to live life fully. To feel alive, we have to *make* experiences – say "Yes," step out of our comfort zone and get started. I agree, the first step is the most difficult, but every journey starts with a first step. Don't think too much when opportunity comes knocking. Don't look for excuses or let other people hold you back from making changes. They often mean good, but they're advice usually stems from their own fear of change.

When I talk about opportunities, I mean the small as well as the monumental ones that present themselves to us. Either way, taking the first step should be your initial reaction. When you have the courage to start, things will develop and fall into place and your journey will find its way. The only sure way to fail is to do nothing at all.

What about fear? Well, as Franklin D. Roosevelt said, "The only thing we have to fear is fear itself." Fear is seemingly the only enemy that can stop us from fulfilling our dreams and taking our lives to the next level. However, what if you choose to make fear your friend? Treat it as the buddy that tells you "Hey, I'm showing up again to alert you that something good is about to happen so you'd better get moving!" I know, fear can be a tough one for some of us. Is it for you? No worries, I have some really helpful pointers on how to face your fears a few chapters away.

For now, try this. Instead of asking yourself "What could happen if I do this?" ask "What will happen if I don't do it?" I assure you, the answers will always be the same. If you get moving and things go wrong along the way, there will always be a solution to put them on the right track. If you don't move, you'll have so much more to lose – perhaps even the experience of your lifetime. You'll get stuck in your life and that would only result in existing, not living. I don't want that for you. Neither do you.

* * *

I believe in leading by example, so here's another life story that illustrates why starting without hesitation is the only way to achieve a dream. When I decided to move to Bali (yes, I've moved around a lot!) I had 2 big dogs that I adored. The only problem was that they don't allow dogs in the country. Now, there was no way I was moving without my dogs. By the same token, there was no way I wasn't moving to Bali. Besides, I just knew that the dogs were going with me. I didn't know how I was going to pull it off, but I decided to just start the journey.

So, I flew from Buenos Aires to Jakarta with my dogs. That worked out okay. Of course, it was no surprise to me when the officials in Jakarta said that they wouldn't allow my dogs into Bali. It seems they have a problem with wild, free-roaming dogs with rabes that bite people and infect them. In any event, I needed to go to Singapore first on visa business and wanted to send the dogs ahead of me. At that moment an idea popped into my head. I called a friend in Bali, who I knew was well-connected, and asked him his advice. It turned out he had a friend who was a policeman. Luckily, policemen are the only ones allowed to bring dogs into the country, as long as they are healthy. I assured my friend that the dogs were in great shape. There was my solution! So, I sent the dogs ahead of me and the policeman took care of them until I arrived a few days later.

Because my dogs were a big part of my life and rated in the top 3 of my value system, they just had to go with me. I wouldn't compromise on that. So, I relied on my faith and knew that the universe would help me if I just took the first step and got on that plane. I didn't know what lied ahead of me, but my faith gave me the courage to move. I'm glad I did, because Bali turned into a wonderful healing time for me. I needed that very much.

There were also times when I started on a journey that didn't work out the way I had planned but led to an unforeseen path that was really good for me. All you need to do is look at my resume to see that – fashion design, real estate, interior design, business management, Chinese medicine, personal coaching and whatever comes next! Believe me, I took the first step with the same conviction for all of these careers and those journeys always led to something totally unexpected, but always great.

For instance, I learned so much in Chinese medicine about human beings and how we connect. Did you know that when you choose a body with weak kidneys this means you're fearful? Yes, everything is connected and nothing exists for no reason.

In any event, I wanted to become an acupuncturist and studied from Buenos Aires. It's all so different than Western diagnostics and I found it enthralling. After I finished my studies I took the first step and traveled to Beijing, not knowing what lied ahead of me. There were challenges there because the language barrier made it impossible to communicate with my patients directly. I therefore used a translator. The amazing thing is that I always somehow connected with these people despite language challenges.

It was very hectic. I had 40 patients and always needed to trust my intuition to make quick decisions. I was so grateful that I had wonderful results and healed many people. So much so that I decided to open my own facility. So, I took the first step and opened up a clinic. The only problem was no one came. You can't have a clinic with no patients, so I eventually closed down. Yes, I was disappointed, but when I look back I know that it needed to be part of my journey and I wouldn't change it for the world. In fact, it led to what I'm doing now. I wanted to be a healer, but instead of doing it with needles I ended up doing it with words.

The point is, even though most of my careers didn't work out the way I wanted, if I hadn't taken the first step I wouldn't have ended up here, loving what I do. It's the moving that counts because you'll see where the detours take you and they'll always bring you to where you need to be. Remember how important faith is in this equation. Faith holds the lamp in front of you and helps you to take the next step even if you can't see very far ahead and don't know where that path is leading. If something is good, the journey may be harder, but you'll know you're on the right course. If something is totally wrong, like sitting in a clinic where no one comes, then you know that soon enough. The signs will all be provided to guide you. Remember, the tools you need are inside yourself.

* * *

In summary, getting started means committing yourself to your decisions and not allowing people to hold you back. It means believing in your own power and taking your life into your own hands. It's also important to realize that getting started is like pushing that very first domino. The others fall in line without you personally having to push them. In other words, the first effort is the hardest. Watch how the universe unfolds everything without any effort from you after your initial start. Isn't that comforting? Of course, at the beginning there's always chaos. Nevertheless, the magic lies in the infinite possibilities in front of you when you take the first step amid that chaos. It's sacred. It's awe inspiring.

Is there a moment of opportunity presenting itself to you right now? Then take your first step. If you don't, the chance will disappear and you'll never get the same opportunity again. Life will keep moving and people and circumstances will change. Then the magical opportunity will be over. It's all up to you and no one can do it for you, so make that commitment and get started now. You can do this. Be in charge with the power of knowing that you can make your dream and ultimate goal a reality.

Wow, just wait and see how your whole attitude will change, as will your interests and priorities. Your life will become more structured and organized and your energy will be more focused than ever before. You might have to make changes to get what you want but as soon as you're on your journey life will unfold its magic, its unpredictability, its infinity.

Be the creator of your journey and the boss of your life. Take control of your productivity and growth. You don't need anyone to do that for you because you're not afraid of life anymore. Welcome your opportunities and just get started. Feel the intensity which comes with the first step. Then you live!

4

NEVER GIVE UP

AFTER I MOVED TO SOUTH AFRICA, I bought a house and began to renovate it. The builder was Muslim, and he had an amazing team working for him. Now, the builder spoke English but the team spoke many different languages, as they do in South Africa. I therefore had a difficult time communicating with them and was very dependent upon the builder for information.

Mind you, this was the first renovation project I took on by myself, and it was in a foreign country to boot. It was scary, to say the least. The biggest challenge I faced was that they didn't have clearly defined construction standards in South Africa. Coming from Europe, I wasn't used to that. For instance, they will walk with you through the house and ask what you need. If you want an electrical outlet on a certain wall and point at it, you cannot assume it will be near the bottom of the wall. It might very well end up in the middle of the wall! I needed to be on top of everything.

One day my builder accompanied me out of town to visit a huge warehouse to decide the types of switches

HOW I FACED MY FEARS

and lights I wanted in my house. I was overwhelmed by the many choices and quite frankly, a bit frustrated. He was very helpful and afterwards, he asked if we could stop somewhere to grab a cup of coffee, so we did. As we sat over our coffees he told me that his wife had passed away a few weeks before that, leaving him with 7 children. Then he proceeded to ask if I would marry him, since we both lived in Cape Town. Honesty, this is one of the few times in my life that I was left totally speechless. He was least 20 years my senior so the idea had never even occurred to me. However, my gut was telling me to be very careful in how I answered him. So, I told him that I would like to think about it. He was agreeable and took me home in his huge pickup.

Still in shock, I called a girlfriend who was Persian and much more familiar with the religious practices and culture of Muslims. She told me that it would be best to tell him that he could be my guardian but not my husband. I thought that was peculiar, but since I didn't know what else to do, I agreed.

I met him at my house and tried my best to explain, with all the charm I could muster, that I preferred him being my guardian instead of my husband. He courteously declined, left and never came back to my house to supervise the construction. From that day he sent his 20-year-old son to manage the renovations instead. I wasn't very comfortable with the situation and was somewhat frightened that this 20-year-old might mess up. I began to have serious doubts and thought a lot about stopping the project. Then I realized that giving up – especially when I had come so far – would be a useless option. So, I decided to take charge of my life and learn more about construction. I even began a long-distance course in Interior Design. It turned out to be extremely useful as I learned so much about electricity, walls, plumbing, etc. With each and every day I became more and more confident in my ability to control and manage the building process myself. The end result was that the house became the best real estate project of my life. I was able to sell it in 2 years and doubled my investment. I also made construction my new career and became a property developer, which I continue to do until this day.

* * *

Walking through life is like riding a bicycle. You have to keep going or else you'll fall. However, you have to be committed. When you're devoted to achieving something, to changing a circumstance in your life or to getting something you really want, you need to promise yourself that you won't give up until you reach your goal. If you signed a contract to develop a property and invested lots of money into it, would you give up on the whole project the moment problems arise? Of course not! Look at your goals the same way. Things are going to happen but giving up is never an option because you've made a commitment.

Now that you're committed, remember that never giving up means making your experiences yourself. Facing the challenges – no matter how difficult they seem at first – and getting over the obstacles. Things will get better, but the most important thing to remember is to keep going. When you get through it all, you'll develop more self-confidence, as I did with my house renovations, and you'll be able to face even bigger challenges ahead. You can take pride in that.

Remember that problems and challenges are a natural part of life. Many of us try to avoid them, but it's really an impossible task. We shouldn't try to escape them because they're actually precious gifts. They help us to grow and become stronger and more creative. Some spiritual teachers say that if you're facing problems in terms of one specific desire or decision you've made, this is a sign that you're becoming prepared for a long-term success or wonderful experience. If something is easy and there's no challenge, chances are it will only last a short time. You probably won't enjoy or appreciate it as much because you didn't fight for it. Even if you feel like you're standing at the edge of an abyss, if you keep moving and don't give up, you won't fall into the darkness. If that seems difficult for you, don't worry because we'll talk more about how you can incorporate the motto "Keep Moving" into your life later on. You'll see how you'll be able to come out of any experience with something really worth the fight. The universe never gives you more than you can handle. You can face it.

* * *

There are different ways of giving up. Some give up on a dream, some on a passion and others on a business venture. Some even give up on their own lives, which is the biggest tragedy of all. What they're missing is faith in the universe, knowing that if something doesn't work out, it's for the better. It's just an obstacle and it must not get in the way of achieving their ultimate goal, which is happiness.

I've had many people say to me, "Verena, I don't want to give up, I just don't think I have the tools." What they aren't realizing is that because they chose their journey they already have everything they need. I always tell them that if they don't know how they'll manage, give it to their higher selves. Say it out loud, "Please help me. I don't know what to do here. Please give me the information and the means I need to achieve my goals." The universe hears you and trust me, the answers are already on their way. Believe in that just as you believe the sun will rise again tomorrow, even if you're sitting in the darkest of night. There's always a solution. Always. You're never alone.

Here's a helpful tip. When you're in despair and facing an impasse, just stop for a moment, clear your mind and focus. Tap into the spirituality and instincts inside you. Do it in silence for an hour. We're not used to that in our Western society. We're constantly bombarded with phone calls, texts, emails and television. We don't find our magic there. Don't give too much energy to what's outside. Just change your focus to inside. Move through it, reconnect with yourself and then wait. After that your mind will become clear and you'll see the big picture. Answers will come, as will energy and creativity. Believe me, you can't find that anywhere outside yourself. Focus inside.

You may say, "I'm trying Verena, but thoughts keep running through my mind and are distracting me." In a lot of ways, our minds are our biggest enemies. When hurdles present themselves, close your mind for a while because it's only there for calculating what it thinks is reality. Shut it down and hear the secret from your higher consciousness. It will reveal the solutions to your problems.

Trust the process and learn what you need to absorb. Discovery takes practice and you'll need to train your skills like an athlete trains his or her muscles. Then you can become more practical. Start asking people if they can help you. Then search the internet for the information you need to solve your problems. We've never had access to information in real time like we do today. Take advantage of that. It's free.

Here's the point: You can trust that if you're supposed to be somewhere you'll either be there, or some better destiny is waiting for you. Have faith in the universe and feel more relaxed. Enjoy your magical journey. Remember, you're much stronger than you think. Don't give up!

FACING YOUR FEARS

FEAR IS AN EXTREMELY STRONG EMOTION AND can have a huge impact on your life. It's very off-putting and in fact, one may find it difficult to differentiate between inner anxiety and real fear. By "real fear" I mean something like what you'd feel when someone holds a gun to your head. That's real danger and the fear makes sense in this instance. However, fear of survival is not what we're talking about here. We're addressing the kind of fear that's an emotional reaction to circumstances that pose no physical harm to us.

By nature, I'm a very fearful person, especially when it comes to security. I've had to face this fear many times in my life and have learned from a coach in Berlin that when this frightful emotion arises it always disappears, one way or another. Even though the problem that causes the anxiety may not be readily resolved, the fear does indeed pass away.

"The Unknown" is at the source of many people's fears. After all, if we knew for sure that everything were going to be all right in the end – and we were able to identify exactly how that was going to take place – there would be no reason to be fearful. Life, of course, does not work that way.

When I was separated from my ex-husband, I moved to Berlin with my daughter to forge a new life. I knew my ex was a top attorney and that divorce negotiations would be tough, but I nevertheless was excited and confident that I would get through it and be happy in my new home. I wasn't worried about my income because my Dad owned part of a huge office building and had promised me that I could live off of the rental income. Sort of an endowment. That would cover me until I got a new job and would then be supplemental income after I started to work. As life would have it, things didn't work out as I planned.

One day my Dad called me and asked if I was alone. He apparently wanted to speak to me in private. My daughter was already on her way to visit her father so I met with my Dad, not thinking it was anything too serious. That's when the bombshell hit. Because he didn't agree with my divorcing my husband, he decided to take back the endowment. He urged me to go back to my ex because he didn't feel I was able to raise my daughter by myself. I felt so betrayed and was devastated.

I remember that I was standing on the balcony of my apartment, maybe 5 or 6 stories up, and was staring at a patch of grass on the ground far below me. This was the only time that I ever thought of taking my life. The fear was overwhelming. I couldn't imagine how I was going to manage the situation. Of course, jumping was not an option. I had a daughter to take care of and valued my life too much. I took a deep breath, composed myself and stepped inside. The fear had passed, even though the problem was still there.

One thing was for certain: I would never go back to my husband. That's when I decided to make fear my friend. I realized it was alerting me that I had to act fast, so I sat down and started to comprise a list of what I could do to immediately bring down my living costs. Moving into a smaller apartment was the first logical step. I therefore decided to speak to the owner of my apartment and told him the truth. He completely understood and allowed me to break the lease with no problems at all. He was about 70 years old – a beautiful soul whose wife cheated on him and had recently left him. We became fast friends. He must have realized how broke I was because he invited me to go sailing with him a couple of Sundays. It was like a free vacation for me, and sorely needed.

When my divorce negotiations started, I wanted to have full custody of my daughter. In the end I gave up all financial support in order to get sole custody. It was worth it to me because it meant that we could live wherever we wanted and were free to start a new life. Things began to fall into place. First, I landed a job in an insurance company, but didn't like it very much. I then received another offer and built up a network marketing business which I eventually sold. After that, my friend offered me a very high paying job at his company in Dusseldorf.

All of this is not to say that my fear of losing security didn't reappear now and again during that period of my life. For years I was fearful of buying anything because everything I earned went toward our living costs. I didn't let the fear paralyze me, though. I realized that, like a buddy, it was telling me that I needed to step up my game, and then I would always just let it pass. (Yes, fear is a friend, but not one you want to hang out with all the time!) I kept moving and it all payed off. With the new job in Dusseldorf, my financial and personal life changed. I met amazing people and my friend was so impressed with me that he offered me a partnership. That afforded me the luxury of buying a beautiful, high-end jeep and other things I wanted. The company even payed for my nanny!

Of course, I don't wish anyone hard times, but I can tell you that experience really made me strong and gave me a sturdier character. Those years made me the woman I am today and I wouldn't change a thing. I became my own soulmate and best friend. I also grew to be more humble and grateful. To this day, when on a date or with friends at an expensive restaurant, I'm so thrilled and thankful to be there, enjoying the glorious food. I can afford it now.

The point is, if I had let the fear stop me from moving forward I would never have realized my dreams. Of course, I had easier options available to me at the time. I could have gone back to my ex-husband – or even looked for another man – to support me. Or I could have asked my Dad if I could work in his company and move back to my little home village. These would have been what seem to be "safer" options, but I would never have become independent. I wanted to make it by myself, and that's what I did. I eventually moved to 3 continents with my daughter and never let fear stop me because I always felt connected to the universe.

* * *

The key to conquering fear is having faith and taking responsibility for your emotions. We'll talk more about how important taking full responsibility for yourself, your actions and your reactions is in the next chapter. You'll see how essential it is in every phase of your life. For instance, if you're always thinking "Woe is me, to whom can I turn to protect me?" it just holds you back. Perhaps your husband wants a divorce, or you're taking a new job or maybe your kids are leaving the nest. Fear pops up and you try to control it or fight it or divert it. That's not going to work. Recognize that fear is trying to tell you something. Live through it, learn from it, and then move on.

I know what you're thinking. "Verena, I get it but where do I begin?" Remember when I said that I went through some training to study how to let fear pass through me? Well, here's what I learned. When the feeling of fear or anxiety arises, first be sure to identify what exactly is making you fearful. Say it aloud. Then, take the time to think about where in your body it's located. Just accept it and say, "Okay, there's where the fear lives." It's as if you were switching a light on it. When you expose it, it goes away.

When people try to not feel fear, ignore it and replace it with constant activity during the day, they think the fear is gone but in reality, it's not. It's with you the moment you go to bed. When you stop running away from it, identify where it lives and then expose it for what it truly is – really feel it and don't judge it – you'll find you can handle it. Trust me, you'll see the fear magically disappear.

It also helps to remember that whatever the situation, you have choices. Make a list of the worst-case scenario, and then think of what Plan B could be. Collect the information you need to make informed choices. You are in control and you can decide what to do to make things better because there are always options available to you. By the way, most of the time a situation is more difficult in our minds than it is in reality. Become aware of that. You chose your journey and you are equipped and protected. Become the creator, the chooser of your possibilities and step into your power. You have the universe backing you. You're never powerless.

So many people are permanently fearful and that makes me sad because this is not why we're here. It drains their energy, takes the light away and makes everything so heavy that they become paralyzed. They know they need to make that difficult call or read the fine print in that important contract but are so fearful that they get stuck and can't move. If only they would stop seeing fear as a monster, but just as a revealing but temporary wave of emotion, they'd get passed it and say "Give me that phone," or "Hand me that contract." They'd get things done and learn from the experience.

To me fear is an opportunity – as I said, a girlfriend that gives me a little kick to get me started so I can be on top of a situation. Indeed, the bigger meaning of fear is that you need to take the next step toward growth. However, we can't allow fear to take over. Be aware that in many ways our society has programmed us to be fearful – financial institutions, insurance companies, you name it. In our subconscious we think, "If I have enough insurance and save enough money, my future will be rosy." We might even think, "Oh, if I get into trouble my parents will be there to help me." No! Leave that thinking behind. You don't need it because you alone have to take responsibility for yourself. Life is life and you accept it for what it is. You don't even know if you will be alive tomorrow, but that's what makes it all so exciting.

* * *

In summary, we now know that only your fears can hold you back from living your dreams. Don't become a slave to those fears. Use them to your advantage. Yes, it may be difficult at first because you're so used to stepping backwards when you're facing fears. However, when you step forward, take a deeper look, make a decision and act upon it, you'll feel empowered. Whether you're a man or woman, you have to embrace your masculine energy. You're capable of it. You just need to change the direction of your focus.

Remember, we can only grow when we leave our comfort zone and become challenged. At the end of the day, fear is only a human emotion. So is happiness. Opt for the latter, and that will make me happy as well.

6

TAKE FULL RESPONSIBILITY FOR YOUR LIFE

AFTER MY DAUGHTER FINISHED HIGH SCHOOL AND moved to New York City to study business, I decided I wanted to move abroad again. I had already lived in Cape Town, South Africa and loved it. However, this time I wanted to be in a similar time zone as my daughter so communicating would be easy. At the same time, I longed to experience an easier lifestyle in a warmer climate. After pondering it for a while, I decided on Argentina.

When I visited Buenos Aires to check it out, there was something that was causing me to feel frightened but I thought it was a normal reaction in a totally new environment. The people seemed to be passionate and proud, which I admired very much. Besides, I always wanted to learn Spanish.

I made my decision to move there fairly quickly. Finding a place to live came quite easily. In fact, I discovered a beautiful apartment in one of the best areas of the city at a perfectly affordable price. I was set up so I moved there shortly thereafter.

In the beginning I found Argentina to be an interesting and vibrant country, but also challenging because it was a little too dangerous for my liking. I did meet some lovely people which eventually grew into close friendships, which is always nice. In short, there were pros and cons to living in Buenos Aires, but I was proud that I made this move and happy to be there.

You know what they say, "Nothing good or bad lasts forever." I wasn't there long before a big presidential election came up and divided the whole country in two. When Mauricio Macri won, he immediately made changes that weren't so popular. Argentina soon became a very expensive country in which to live. What's more, it became even more of a dangerous place to be because the economy, which was facing huge deflation, was causing many people to lose their jobs. They were therefore becoming desperate and more apt to commit crimes.

One of the things that impressed me most was how fast things and people change when politics make a great shift in a country. You could see suffering in people's faces. Many, many more folks were homeless and even in the more well-to-do areas I noticed that people's clothing didn't look as new and fashionable as before. Folks were even driving more aggressively, so crossing the streets became dangerous. Everyone seemed angry.

I grew to be unhappy and realized I had made a mistake moving there. I mean, how could I build a business and a personal life in this place? It would take years before the economy would bounce back again. I'm also a very sensitive person and the anger and suffering in people's faces were causing me to be unhappy and frustrated. I was also frightened to move around the city.

No, I made the wrong decision and my first reaction was to blame myself for ignoring my intuition which was warning me of impending danger when I first arrived in Buenos Aires. Then I started to blame the circumstances that brought me there.

When I got over my initial reaction, I changed my point of view. I saw clearly that nobody forced me to make this decision. I made it all by myself but at least I had lots of new experiences, met some great friends and learned another language. Everything changes sooner or later and when I accepted that I realized I had to work on a new plan. But what to do? Well, I always wanted to be a healer and was interested in Chinese medicine, so I began to study it and found it fascinating.

I eventually went to Beijing to work in a clinic and finish my practical studies in order to become a practitioner of traditional Chinese medicine. While there I realized that even though my daughter and I would be living in completely different time zones, we would make it work and stay connected as much as we wanted. I found myself very happy to be living on yet another continent.

As you know, my career as a Chinese medicine clinician was short-lived. This time I didn't blame myself or circumstances for that decision. I took responsibility for it and sat down to make another plan of action. That's when I began to think of Bali. Since I first visited there I had always imagined what it would be like to live in Indonesia but never thought that would be possible. So, I started to research and within 6 months I was on a plane, headed for a new life in this enchanting place.

Moving to Bali was a big challenge for me, but I was ready for it and have to say that my experiences in Argentina were part of the reason. Once again it became clear to me that at the end of the day, everything happens for a reason and it all guided me to the next level. I just needed to take responsibility for my decision and move on.

* * *

Statistics say that 70% of the decisions we make are wrong. Successful people reflect on what went awry, asking themselves what they could have done differently to achieve more positive results. They then learn from the experience, never make that particular mistake again and move on.

Unfortunately, most people don't like to take full responsibility for their lives because it's so much easier to blame someone else for mistakes. Until they learn to change this behavior, they'll always be their parents' child, looking for someone to take responsibility for them – in other words, rescue them. This doesn't work, though. It's only when we stop blaming our partners, or a circumstance or even the government for something that's making us unhappy in our lives that we can truly free ourselves.

For instance, if a woman finds out that her husband is cheating on her, her first reaction will almost certainly be one of anger and despair. "Oh, he ruined my life!" She'll blame him for his infidelity to avoid feeling shame. Of course, her husband is a lousy human being, but to get caught up in blaming him will only keep her in a position of powerlessness. She'll remain the victim and will only achieve handing the power over to him.

The woman needs to change her position. She should sit down and admit to herself, "Hey, no one held a gun to my head when I married this man. It was my decision and it was a terrible one." Then she'd be taking responsibility for her life and this would be her first mature step toward a healthy state-of-being, both inside and out. She's released, she's free.

Now she can get on top of the situation. "I need to speak with him and get into couples' therapy. If that doesn't work, I'll leave him." At this point, the power shifts back to her. She's once again in a position to create her own life. Sure, she made a mistake, but so what? She's going to correct it and move on because she's the manager of her own life. She now knows that she is the temple of her soul and therefore responsible for getting her problems solved.

We can all live this way because we are truly in control of our own lives. Also remember not to be so hard on yourself when you take responsibility for a bad decision or mistake. Learned to forgive yourself. After all, you forgive others so easily, so why not afford yourself the same courtesy and love?

* * *

An interesting thing about taking responsibility for your life and all of your decisions is that it changes your relationships for the better. All those feelings of being powerless and victimized melt away as you start to live as a responsible person in society. Gone are the conscious or subconscious blockages or patterns that keep you in a state of forever depending upon someone. People will notice that and even be attracted to it. They'll want to be with you and help you on your journey.

This is particularly noticeable in marriages and relationships. When people take full responsibility for their lives they begin to act more like adult partners instead of constantly sending out passive, manipulative energy. For instance, if you want to travel to Asia but your boyfriend doesn't because he's not crazy about being in a plane for such a long distance, realize that you have a decision. Take responsibility. Perhaps if you stay back you'll only grow to regret it and resent him. Instead, you can opt to take the trip alone. If the relationship falls apart because you took a vacation without him, the partnership had more serious problems to begin with.

Remember, you *are* in control. Take your power back and then life will become exciting because you're creating it. You don't need anyone to make your life interesting. When you're not happy, make a plan. No one can walk your way. Don't be a victim. You're responsible for everything. You'll empower yourself because you're the master of your destiny. Remember, the journey is the target.

7

ASK THE UNIVERSE

AFTER MY DIVORCE, I HAD VERY LITTLE money to work with and it was so difficult to find a job in Berlin. We didn't even have many friends who could connect me with the opportunities I needed. My daughter and I were therefore living off of my savings, but they were depleting quickly.

I did finally manage to start a business selling diet products and health supplements for an American company in Germany. However, the first month's commissions weren't enough to make ends meet. I needed another 500 Euros to pay the rent. At that point I decided to pray a lot and ask the universe for help. A couple of days later I remembered that my Dad had given my daughter a savings account when she was born. I didn't remember how much was in there, so I searched for the book and found it. I couldn't believe my eyes. There were exactly 1000 German Marks in the account, which was the equivalent to 500 Euros!

I asked my daughter if I could borrow it and told her I would pay her back as soon as I could. She was so little and sweet and happy to help me. So, I took the book to the bank to get the 500 Euros, but the teller gave me 1000 instead. She obviously didn't realize that there were German Marks and not Euros in the account. Normally I would have said something because I'm a very honest person. However, this time I had the feeling that the universe wanted me to keep the money, so I did.

The extra 500 Euros meant a great deal to me. I was excited about the gift that the universe gave me and derived so much positive energy from it. I didn't feel so lonely and helpless anymore because I realized that the universe had my back. Feeling renewed, I paid my rent, saved the rest of the money and focused 100 percent on my new business. I asked people for advice on how to be a better salesperson and learned something new every day. I was unstoppable and quickly became one of the top 10 salespeople in my region.

I eventually received another offer to sell a DVD and made a successful presentation to over 4,500 people in Frankfurt. I was thrilled! After I asked the universe for help and saw the miracle it bestowed up me, I started to trust again. It's amazing how much a person changes when someone believes in him or her. The universe believed in me. It's all I needed.

* * *

It's crucial to ask the universe for help whenever you're facing a challenge, big or small. If you've never done this before, start with something small, like asking for a parking spot on your way to a destination where spots are few and far between. You'll be surprised to see how well it works!

Then get into the habit of doing it for everything you want. Let it become your personal tool to create your own reality.

When you trust that there is something bigger than you, like a "universal mind," you'll be able to connect with it and realize that we all have a direct telephone line to it. All we have to do is call. You'll be amazed at how much it will boost your confidence in knowing that you can and will handle everything in your life.

I used to get signs from the universe when I was facing problems. I'd see the words, "take it easy," or "be positive" or "everything is going to be fine." Sometimes I'd see them all in one day, but my mind would reject it and think "shut up!" My inner feelings and belief patterns changed when I received those extra Euros from the universe after asking for help. When I believed that the universe was backing me, I felt so motivated and full of trust that nothing could stop me. The same will happen for you. You just need to open yourself up and start communicating with universe.

∗ ∗ ∗

Many people ask me how this big, infinite universe can understand or even be aware of their comparatively tiny problems and help fix them. They cannot imagine that with all the grandness of the universe they have the power within themselves to ask and receive. They feel inconsequential, but nothing can be further from the truth. They need to stop using their minds, which are basically calculators. Their minds can only analyze – this is black, this is white, this is brown. There is so much more.

There are a few practical tips on how to start connecting with the universe and ask for your heart's desire. The first thing to do is to be absolutely clear as to what you really want. For instance, a woman may ask the universe to bring her the perfect partner so she can marry and have a secure life. However, she may still be longing for an exciting life full of parties and travel, free of responsibilities and children. She's sending out mixed messages to the universe and will most probably not get her wish until her value system is in line.

You also see this a lot with celebrities. On the one hand they ask for fame but on the other hand want their privacy and don't like being chased by paparazzi. Again, mixed messages. So, the first step to asking the universe for something is to understand yourself, your values and what you really and truly want. How do you do that? Well, take time to examine what outside influences are possibly skewing your desires. Perhaps your partner or society is telling you that this is what you *should* want. Look inside. Is it true? It may not be.

My parents declared that I should get married, and what's more, told me that that's what *I* wanted. I therefore tried marriage three times until I discovered, when seeing couples with their families, that I really didn't want that at all. I'm too free-spirited and could never live this way. I'm happy being unmarried (and thrilled that I have a daughter) so now I no longer send out a confusing message to the universe where relationships are concerned. A lot of it has to do with setting goals. Not sure how to do that? Don't worry, I've devoted a full chapter to it later on. For now, suffice it to say that you need to understand what it is you truly desire, and be sure it's in line with your value system.

The minute you're clear about what you really want, then you can start communicating with the universe and feel that direct connection. You'll immediately trust that what you're asking for will come. After all, when you order something online does it ever occur to you that it won't be delivered? No, of course it will! It's the same with ordering a desire from the universe.

I found that sometimes it helps if I don't get too detailed in what I'm asking the universe to bring me. Instead of asking for an apartment in a certain location, at a certain price and with so many square feet, I ask for an apartment where I'll be happy. I might be located in an area I didn't even know existed. For some people this is a challenge because they think that they know all the specific details of what they want. Well, remember my Chinese clinic? The universe told me that it wasn't really what I wanted and guess what, it was right! So be open to asking the universe to bring you fulfillment in your business, family and financial life and it will come to you in ways you might never have imagined. Maybe you'll find an investor to back your business, or someone will leave you money. You might even meet the man of your dreams at a party you almost didn't attend. You never know!

Remember when we talked about how helpful walking away from a problem for a short period of time can be? Something inevitably happens in a few hours or a day later that brings a solution. It's the same way with asking the universe for help. Just say "Please fix this for me" and then focus on something totally different. I guarantee you'll get an impulse – a message – that will help you on your way. Perhaps something will tell you to call someone or pick up a book or surf the internet. Whatever the impulse is directing you to do, don't hesitate. Just do it. You'll find the solution.

Another practical tip is to have patience. When you ask the universe for something, remember that there may be other people and circumstances that are involved so it might take some time for the universe to work it all out so everyone is happy. Whatever you do, don't have doubts. Remember, once you ask the universe for help, your order is being processed – just like that online purchase. If one day you ask for a Porsche, but the next day your boss says something that frightens you into believing you may lose your job, don't say "I won't be able to afford the car so I don't want it anymore." The car is already being delivered to you, and the universe will be asking you "Is it yes or no?" Again, mixed messages can really hold things up!

A good way to assist the universe in bringing you your dream is to make a vision board. At one point in Bali I realized that my time was done there and decided that my next home would London. There were challenges, though. It's more expensive to live in this beautiful city and I had two big dogs that were too old to move. You know how much I loved those dogs – they were my loving companions in Cape Town, Buenos Aires and now in Bali. I didn't know exactly what to do with my dogs but I didn't let the challenges get in my way. I created a vision board in December with different sites and streets of London on it. I put the board on my cell phone and laptop and looked at it constantly and by June I was living in London. It turned out that my best friend in Bali offered to take the dogs so I knew they would have a happy home. In fact, I see the kids playing with them on Instagram all the time. The dogs are happy and the solution was perfect. All of the logistics worked out, even though it was a tremendous move. The universe is so awesome!

* * *

Imagine that the universe is always sending out a vibration. That energy is there for you to connect to. Of course, it's not always easy. We're often times surrounded by negative energy emulating from other people. Sometimes from within ourselves, as well. That only pulls us down and we end up attracting more negative energy in the form of people that aren't good for us or circumstances we don't want. That frustrates us and we become upset. But we do have a choice. When we open up and become aware of the universal mind and energy, we can focus on a better energy.

How can we achieve that when we're angry or sad? Through conscious actions. Put on some music, play with your dog, hug your kids. Go to the gym, do some yoga or take a walk in the park. Or perhaps just stop in your favorite café for a coffee, juice or tea. Little things like these can make monumental shifts in your outlook. Smile and let go of the negative energy. Rise up within and your outside world will change.

As the master of your soul and existence you have the ability to be a positive force, so insist on surrounding yourself with positive people as well. You have the absolute power of the universe backing you. Harness that power and ask the universe for immediate, concrete help and know that it will indeed come to you because you deserve it. You'll become the ruler of your thoughts and emotions and you'll hold the cards of your life in your hands. That's the awesomeness that is you, a child of the universal mind!

8

TRUST YOUR INTUITION

WHILE LIVING IN CAPE TOWN, MY DAUGHTER would travel to Europe during the holidays and summers to spend some time with her father. Since she was away a whole month during summer vacation, I would usually plan something special for me. For instance, one summer I received an impulse to write a book. I was really inspired and the words just seemed to fly from my hands to my laptop. While I was working on chapters that discussed issues of fear, loneliness, attraction, love and freedom, I received yet another impulse. This time my intuition was telling me that I should travel to Thailand. My mind was telling me that this was crazy, especially when I had planned to use the time my daughter was away to write a book. However, I had begun to learn how to ignore my mind so I trusted my intuition and booked a flight to Thailand.

Before leaving, I sent 12 chapters to a friend of mine who was a professional editor. I figured he could work on the book while I enjoyed Thailand. It was a beautiful trip, and I was so inspired by the country, people and culture that

I ended up taking 800 photos! Before returning, my friend emailed me saying that he was impressed with my spiritual book and asked if he could send it to a friend who was a huge publisher in South Africa. I was thrilled and honored!

While I was en route home, the publisher sent me a message asking for a meeting in Cape Town. I took the meeting, and while discussing the book I had written, I also showed him some of my Thailand photos. He was so inspired that we created a beautiful coffee table book that was published in three languages and available in South Africa through a company similar to Amazon. Imagine, all this started with only two messages from my intuition and turned into something I could never have imagined.

* * *

I like to view intuition as everything we don't analyze. It's very silent, more like an impulse. Think of it not like a proper sentence, but like a word. It's also very shy and doesn't speak to us very often. You can also view intuition as being your inner compass. It guides you through your life because it knows the bigger plan.

You need to train yourself to be quiet and open to hear your intuition. Only then will you realize that it's speaking to you and that you can trust it. The challenge is that intuition comes fast, but our lives are also moving quickly. Because it moves in like a flash, you need to put action behind intuition and work fast.

After experiencing a disappointment, have you ever said to yourself, "I knew that was going to happen"? That knowledge and wisdom was your intuition, and it came so rapidly that you weren't trained to hear it. Plus, your mind can be so strong that it tends to ignore intuition and instead opts to analyze and act upon the analytics. We're so conditioned to this behavior that we've forgotten the difference between what our minds think and what our intuition is telling us. That's when we make wrong moves.

The fact is, our intuition speaks to us the very first moment a situation appears. It comes in the form of an impulse, impression or feeling rather than a thought. Of course, that's when the mind steps in and starts analyzing again. So, we need to learn how to ignore what the mind is telling us and listen to our intuition. However, we have to hone that talent with practice, or else we'll be confused and not know what to act upon.

That brings us to another challenge, which is being able to differentiate between the voice of our intuition and feelings such as excitement or fear. These emotions often feel like impulses and can be easily misunderstood. As I said, it takes practice.

You'll find that living in line with your intuition saves you a lot of energy, gives you power and connects you to yourself and your life's purpose. Again, you need to separate intuition from your mind, trust in it and most importantly act upon it immediately. This is often the most difficult part of the process because we're so easily prone to insecurity in our decisions and feel more comfortable just sitting back and not doing anything at all. However, if you act on your intuition right away you'll commit to that inner voice and become empowered knowing that everything you need is inside yourself.

* * *

HOW I FACED MY FEARS

Your intuition speaks to you in some of the most surprising ways. For example, if you're in the bathroom or a taxi and an idea about making a film that takes place in Antarctica pops into your head, you should jot it down. Of course, your mind will immediately tell you that you can't do that. Antarctica would be too harsh a climate in which to make a film. How could I ever pull that off? Ignore it. When you get a message like that, believe me it's bigger than your mind could ever fathom.

No one and nothing can guide you like your intuition because it sees your whole life, the big picture and your soul's journey. It knows where you come from and where you want to go. Your abilities, your experience, everything. It happens so fast and it's easy to ignore but when we learn to listen to it and stick with it, intuition will always lead us to the best decision. It guides us, it saves us, it protects us.

I can tell you that I definitely practice what I preach! When I meet someone and have an intuition that I cannot trust him, even though he seems to be a nice person, I heed the message. When I see something that looks delicious at a buffet but something tells me not to eat it, I don't. I put action – or inaction – behind my intuitions, however crazy it may seem.

For instance, I was waiting to board an airplane with my daughter when I had the feeling that everything and everyone around me looked strange. I can't explain why. Even the plane was late. While waiting, my daughter broke her tooth eating some hard candy. That was it! Too many signs for me so I cancelled the trip, even though my family was waiting for us in Germany. I found out that the plane had arrived safely, but perhaps something else would have happened to us if we had taken it. Who knows, maybe a fight with my family or a taxi accident. I don't know, but I'm glad I trusted my intuition instead of putting myself in a situation that might have caused a big problem, and a lot of energy to get out of.

If I recounted every instance my intuition saved the day, this book would be way too long! What I can say is that when I moved to Africa, Buenos Aires, Indonesia and now London, I don't know what I would have done without my intuition. When I was in Buenos Aires I was in dangerous situations all the time and relied upon my intuition constantly. Should I go here, should I go there? Don't take that street, take another. You have to be in tune to your intuition. I'm German and come from a culture where if we have an appointment, even if it's snowing and dangerous to walk, we do it and walk anyway. I had to change that habit, listen to my intuition and say, listen, we need to cancel this appointment for now. It's too dangerous to travel.

* * *

So how do you start following your intuition? Well, you don't have to wait for some monumental life decision. Start with simple things. If you're looking for a new doctor, go to several websites and see what your intuition is telling you. By the way, I don't look at reviews. What's good for one person may not necessarily work for me.

So, after browsing, did one of the websites speak to you? Then make an appointment. When you meet the doctor, listen closely to your intuition the moment you greet each other. If you don't have a good feeling, put action behind it and graciously walk away. This is your life so take responsibility, even if people think you're crazy for following your intuition when things on the outside seem to be in order. You're inside is telling you that something is not right so don't worry about it. Do it and grow because you have the power and are in control.

Here's another possible scenario. Let's say you hired a lawyer to help you in a difficult situation. As you're sitting in a meeting with him, you start to yawn and are becoming more and more tired even though you had a full night's rest. Bingo, that's a sign that you most probably should be looking for another lawyer. Sounds crazy? I can tell you that I have never in my life had a bad feeling about a situation that turned out in a good way. When I didn't follow my intuition because I was too shy, too polite or too embarrassed, it never turned out well. Just be direct, without blaming, and say "I don't think this is going to work out."

Intuition comes in all sorts of manifestations. Just be sure you differentiate between real impulses and your emotions. Remember, we chose the souls that walk with us in this life long before we got here. Your intuition recognizes these souls when they come your way, even though your conscious mind doesn't. Listen!

* * *

In many ways, intuition is your best friend. It will guide you in a way which is in tune with your entire life's journey. It knows your soul's plan and what your soul wants to experience. Your mind is certainly not your enemy. It knows the math and facts you need to function. However, it can be a detriment when you give it too much power. Our minds often remind us of previous, bad experiences or give us excuses to hold back and not forge ahead toward our destiny.

You can always be sure that where your heart leads you'll find your true way. Ignore analytics and logistics when intuition speaks. Let go, trust and act on what it's telling you.

I often ask myself "Where do I want to be 10 years from now?" An experienced and interesting woman who has something valuable to say and give, or a woman who thinks back and says, "What would have happened if I had done it another way?" I opt for no regrets. You can too, because you are connected to something much bigger. Inside you are all the gifts the universe has bestowed upon you. Intuition is one of those precious gifts. Tap into it and be inspired.

9

FIND PEACE IN BEING ALONE

NO ONE WANTS TO BE ALONE. IN fact, for many, being alone is a very difficult challenge. In a way I understand it because we are conditioned to think that way. However, I've come to learn that when a person is comfortable being alone, he or she has received one of the biggest gifts life can offer.

The truth is, we're never really alone because we have ourselves. Before we incarnate into our lives, there are no boundaries. We are all connected and are all on the same energy level. We are one. When we decide to become a person, boundaries appear but they allow us to make individual experiences that we couldn't create when we were one with other souls. That gives us freedom of choice and it's a joyous thing. The trouble is, we forgot this. Psychology teaches us that we feel disconnected when we come into this world and subconsciously want to reconnect to our previous state of being. Therefore, from the moment we come out of the safe wombs of our mothers into this seemingly cold world we are forever trying to find our soulmates – lovers, friends, teachers – so we won't be alone. This, however, is an illusion. In fact, it's impossible.

If we could really become one with a soulmate, then we could never shape special experiences in our own lives and achieve everything we desire. That's what we're here for. What we really should be doing is to find a way to become whole again – the way we were before we got here. We'll only find it in ourselves, not in other people. That requires being alone at times. What you'll discover is that when you consciously choose to be alone, you'll become free. It gives you the chance to deeply connect to yourself and find peace with your inner child. That's when you'll feel whole and satisfy that deep longing to be as you were before you were born.

* * *

People will often do anything but look to themselves to feel whole. Industry wants us to buy things to feel complete and satisfied. This designer handbag will make me feel whole. That donut will fulfill my soul. Society teaches us that if we go to that important social event – even if we're not interested in attending – we'll feel whole. Marry that rich guy – even if you don't love him – and you'll feel complete. Nothing can be further from the truth. These things often leave us feeling empty if we haven't first learned to reconnect with ourselves first. When we do connect with our inner selves, we'll learn that we don't have to depend on other persons or things to give us the peace and "wholeness" that we need. Be whole and love yourself first, then you can then enjoy the expensive bag and indulgent donut for the right reasons. Don't marry the guy you don't love, though! Well, you would know not to because you'd be whole and love yourself too much for that anyway.

When people haven't been able to be alone and be comfortable in their own skin, they often mess up partnerships. People will stay in unhealthy relationships because they're afraid of being by themselves. It's not honest and it's definitely not from the heart. Worse than that, it keeps them in a holding pattern. They're stuck, and not in a happy place. If they would only learn to be comfortable with whom they truly are, they would find peace in taking responsibility for their lives. (Remember how important that is?) They'd be able to take action, communicate with the universe and be the masters of their own lives.

Have you ever heard of the expression, "Swim next to me and we'll both get there, but if you hold on to me we'll both drown"? What this is saying to me is that when you can truly be alone with yourself and learn to be whole, then and only then will you be able to completely share yourself with someone else. That will make for a healthy, happy relationship with friends, family, coworkers and lovers.

Share yourself with you first and then you can share yourself with others unconditionally and without manipulation. The energy will be crystal clear, like in a business. I deliver you this, you deliver me that, and this is our exchange rate. Then the energy flows deeply and cleanly because the motivation is clear. I'm not with you because I'm afraid of being by myself. I'm with you because I want to be. I am me, you are you, and we're going to walk – or swim – together in a healthy, fulfilling friendship or relationship.

HOW I FACED MY FEARS

* * *

It took me years to learn the benefits of being alone. When I started to study fashion design, I was like a maniac! I was constantly inviting friends to come over and often asked my girlfriends to stay overnight. I just hated being by myself. When I did find myself alone, I would fill my hours with work, cleaning my apartment, shopping for groceries or clothes – anything to keep busy. I really felt disconnected from myself.

During this time in my life, I had a very close relationship with one of my girlfriends. She was an extremely spiritual, amazing person whom I loved and respected very much. One day, while studying together, she told me in a very warm-hearted and empathetic way that she felt a bit used by me. I didn't understand this at first until she explained that she sensed I was using our relationship to fill a void in my life. She recommended that I speak with a psychologist about healing therapies that would help me to become friends with my "inner child" and find the peace I was seeking. I resisted at first, but then realized she was right.

I made an appointment with the therapist and while sitting in the waiting room I had a panic attack. This shocked me and was difficult to experience, but I realized that the fear was telling me that I needed to change something in my life. I finally gained control and had my first session. I talked about myself for an hour, after which the psychologist recommended me to a therapy clinic. This traumatized me. Was I really so crazy?

Well, I got over my initial reaction and realized that I wasn't crazy at all. I was normal. In fact, that day changed my life. I decided that the clinic wasn't right for me, so I made a

conscious effort to find time to be alone and reconnect with my "inner child." It made all the
difference in the world. I really enjoyed my time alone and it helped me to appreciate being with others more. Even after spending time with someone, I would reflect – by myself – on the conversation or experience and that made it all so much more valuable.

* * *

So, once you've decided that you want to spend time alone, where do you start? Well, think about your lifestyle. Are you feeling like everyone wants something from you every moment of the day? Do you approach Friday and realize your weekend is filled with appointments, leaving no time for you?

Ask yourself, "Do I really want to be running around, doing chores and having dinner with friends Friday, Saturday and Sunday? Do I feel obligated? Of course, everyone has responsibilities, especially where family is involved. Therefore, you need to find a balance. You don't necessarily want to be alone for a week straight. You're just wanting to take time during your day to reconnect and need do it on a regular basis. Explain it to your friends or family and they'll understand. In fact, they'll benefit from it because your state of being will be affected in such a positive way.

Lots of people ask me if being alone means sitting in a room by themselves, doing nothing but thinking. Well, sometimes that's useful but I recommend creating some meaningful, enjoyable time alone. Respect yourself and your body and do something you really like and enjoy. Meditate, read a book, listen to music, go the museum or just take a long walk. Whatever you do, do it by yourself. Don't try hard to be alone, just enjoy it and you'll find that you'll magically begin to reconnect with yourself.

It's especially important to let a partner know before you enter a relationship that you'll be needing this time alone now and then. Don't be frightened of this. For example, if you'd like to take a trip alone, don't feel like your partner will leave you or cheat while you're away. That's just obsessive thinking. Remember, it's only when you love yourself that you can really love someone else. Your partner will benefit from it.

By the way, if he does leave, you will still love him and survive with this love. Feel the heart pain and set him free. Just say "I love you and you need to decide if it's good to be with me, but this has nothing to do with my heart and thankfulness for the time we've had together. If your ego tries to get in the way, tell it to shut up. Cry, feel it and let him go. If he comes back, it was meant to be.

* * *

It's amazing what learning to be alone will do for your social life. Sounds odd, right? Being alone helps you to be successful in not being alone. Unfortunately, many people try to fill their lives with work, people and relationships and find themselves failing. That's mainly because manipulation is involved and they're not going into their work environment and entering relationships for the right reasons. They need to stop searching for something outside themselves to feel complete and discover what they need deep inside. Being alone can help them do that. Then when they are in the company of friends, coworkers or lovers, manipulation disappears because they're not using someone to avoid be alone. They find themselves feeling free to enjoy being with people without being dependent upon them.

Like so many of the topics we've discussed in this book thus far, being alone gives you the power to live life the way you want, in your own style and at your own pace. Take charge and become more and more connected to whom you are inside to achieve ultimate "wholeness." Then go out into the world and attract good people to you like a magnet. Make your companionship a valuable commodity and become sought after only by people you respect.

Also open yourself up to you instead of always being available for other people. Your time is valuable, so take the reins and let people know that. They'll appreciate it because when you do spend time with them, you'll be doing it heartily and with joy. Create this balance in your life and be sure about your decisions, feelings and opinions. Take action, be grounded and stable, and watch how your aura will change in a positive, awe-inspiring way.

By the way, after spending so much time alone all these years, I've found that I'm my best girlfriend. I find that very empowering!

10

TOMORROW IS ANOTHER DAY

WE'VE HEARD IT SO OFTEN THAT I think we may have become immune to the power of the statement, "Tomorrow is another day." It usually pops up when people are lost as to a solution on how to solve a problem today, or if they're depressed about a situation in their lives. Whatever the circumstance, the statement pops up when there is stress involved. The thing is, we often manufacture all the stress we're experiencing ourselves. Our minds create scenarios which we think are reality and we're often unable to see the bigger picture or a way out.

Part of the problem is that in our Western culture we tend to strive for perfection. To many of us, perfection means seizing the moment and acting immediately and decisively when we are confronted with a difficult decision or circumstance. Society puts pressure on us to act this way, making us feel that we are failures if we hesitate. In effect, we've become sort of like marionettes at the hands of societal pressures as they manipulate us to act certain ways.

Time also plays a pivotal role in the way we behave since it's so limited and valuable. Because of our perception of time as always fleeting, we are easily put under pressure to make quick decisions even though we feel that we're not ready. That's when so many mistakes are made.

This is where we must think of the phrase, "Tomorrow is another day." In fact, I recommend that you make it your mantra in times of difficult decisions or when facing forks in the road of your journey. The phrase reminds us of the real essence of life and takes the pressure off. For instance, when you're faced with a situation that requires a solution which is impossible for you to ascertain today – or if you feel you're just not confident enough to decide at the moment – that's a red flag. Stop, calm down and look at everything clearly and realistically. You'll realize that you're not going to die if you step back for a few hours, or maybe even sleep on it, and then face the challenge tomorrow. Give yourself a break. You need more time.

* * *

When we take heed of the phrase "Tomorrow is another day" it will help us to create better time management in our professional and personal lives. Of course, we have to keep up with the pace of modern society. There are situations when swift and immediate decision-making is necessary, especially in times of emergency or crisis. This is where you do the best you can, and believe me, in times of danger, your instincts will guide you. These situations are extreme, though. For the most part, even though everything around us is moving quickly and we need to keep up, we must also act with confidence and professionalism. That's the way leaders conduct themselves.

Timing is a very important factor in the process. If there's a delay in your action because you need to sleep on a decision, you can be sure that there's a reason for it. Today is probably not the right time because information is missing which can only be delivered tomorrow. Trust life, trust this philosophy of timing, act in line with your abilities, and always be professional.

I learned a lot about this in Indonesia, especially in Bali, where it's very inappropriate to behave in a hectic, impulsive manner. When people come together to discuss business or anything else, they always act with patience and a gentle attitude. There it's considered totally unprofessional to come straight to the point, or to set a deadline for important decisions which only prove to put everyone under pressure.

Of course, coming from a Western perspective, I was often challenged by this when I first arrived there. In my business dealings with these lovely people, I would feel that I didn't have the time to waste and needed to get everything done faster. I was becoming a nervous wreck!

In time, though, I learned how useful this approach to business was. These folks taught me that if you take time to talk, discuss and decide on an issue properly, you always had better, sounder business results. Instead of dreading business meetings, I began to enjoy them and even looked forward to them. This is also a much healthier lifestyle and I found that my body and mind benefited from it tremendously.

* * *

There are three useful steps that will help you to manage every challenge which just cannot be handled today. First, *Take Assessment of the Situation*. Clearly define what the problem is by jotting down all the facts and issues you're facing. Think about why you're not able to decide on this right now.

The next step is to *Get What You Need to Make the Decision*. This is where timing is so important, because you need to make the time to communicate that more clearly to yourself and people around you. Talk to your partner, husband or even your client. Tell them you need some fact-finding time before you can make a move. That may come tomorrow or the next day. I know they'll understand and respect you even more because you're behaving responsibly and professionally.

The final step then, of course, is to *Remind Yourself that Tomorrow is Another Day*. Just do today what you can so you'll feel in harmony with your values and your life conception and then let the problem go. Walk away from it and concentrate on something else. We've seen before how effective this can be in making decisions, both big and small. You'll be so surprised how tomorrow will bring you information and possibilities that just weren't available today. You'll receive an email, stumble upon an article, hear something on television or just have an impulse – maybe even a dream. Then you'll possess what you need to go back to yesterday's challenge and will be ready to make your decision – or handle and manage it – whatever the case may be. Good things need time to develop so trust that the universe is at work in your life. We are protected and guided and indeed, tomorrow will bring another bright and beautiful day with endless possibilities.

SET GOALS

Could you imagine setting out to build a house without an architectural plan? Of course not! It's the same thing with life. If you want to achieve something special, you need to create a clear plan and have in your sights something or someplace to reach. Without doing this, it would be like driving a car with a navigation system but never entering a final destination. You have a built-in navigation system within yourself – you just need to remember to enter the destination data!

The first step is to discover what it is you really want. We've talked about how difficult this can be at times because we're so very influenced by people and circumstances around us. Parents tell you that you want this, teachers tell you that you want that, society tells you that you want the other thing. It's all very confusing and often misleading.

In addition, our belief systems, behavioral patterns and education often determine what we *think* we desire. If you want to discover what you really want to achieve, it would be best to sit down and make a proper list. Begin by asking yourself exactly why you want to achieve a particular goal. Why is it so desirable for you? The answers might surprise you because, as we said, we are all so influenced by our surroundings that it often clouds what we really long for.

I knew the son of an extremely successful hotelier in Germany who didn't want into the family business. In fact, to his family's dismay, he opened up a flower shop. High Society was shocked, but he became the happiest person in the whole family. It doesn't matter what you want. If you desire to collect stamps and this is your passion, go for it. When you have something that really draws you, make it your goal. It makes no difference how unattainable it is or how unrealistic it feels. It's what you want.

So, when it comes to getting in touch with our true dreams, desires and goals we are stepping into a very important process of self-discovery. You need to reach deep within yourself to find out what really makes you happy. What force drives you? What gives you goosebumps and makes you really excited? When you do find that something, then ask yourself why you want to achieve it. Be sure it's for the right reasons. If it's because you're afraid of something else, you need to reexamine. Are you're striving for it because of love or fear? Many times, our actions are based on these two extremes of our emotional scale. They can provide you with a great indication as to why you strive so hard to achieve certain things or experiences.

Once you're sure of a certain desire and goal, let's say it's professional, then go back and search deep inside to discover goals that will cover every other aspect of your life. Ask yourself what kind of relationship you'd like to have. Monogamous, open, kids? Where would you like to travel? Your own country or internationally? How do you want to look? Is it your desire to lose weight, change the color of your hair, or possibly have plastic surgery?

The next step, which is to discover the emotions each goal triggers in you, might be more challenging but is just as important. Ask yourself what you are feeling when you think of the specific goals you want to achieve. Once you're in touch with them, these emotions are significant because they act as a shortcut to realizing your dreams. They'll help you to reach those goals even faster because they'll always be there to tap into and energize you while you're headed toward your targets. Keep these emotions alive always. They'll fuel you on your journey.

* * *

So, you know you need to identify the good feelings that are attached to your goals. You also know that you need to tap into them as a shortcut to achieving those goals. The thing of it is getting in touch with emotions is easier for some than others. However, there's a practical way to do it.

Search for things that you can associate with your goals to help you to recreate the particular, exciting feelings those dreams evoke in you. That could be anything from an image to music to a quote, or even just a word. Whatever it is that makes you feel as though you've already achieved your goal, tap into it frequently. It's so important.

Then start living with it. Imagine in your mind's eye that you already achieved what you want. Act as if you have it, talk as if you have it, be as if you have it. Allow the energy to embrace you. I promise, you'll walk differently and your body language will change. All types of interesting and even amazing people will be attracted to you and you'll begin to experience circumstances you never thought you would or even could encounter. This is key because the universal mind will tune into your frequency and will realize the goal for you. All you need to do is to step into this vibration and walk with it and the outside world will respond to it. It's magical!

For example, if you want to get married, ask for an appointment at a nice boutique and dry on some wedding dresses that strike your fancy. Feel it, choose one and put it on hold. Dive into the joy you're feeling and keep the emotion alive. It will boost an inner sensation that will say to you, "You are a bride." That sensation will attract your wedding day sooner that you can imagine.

This is an astonishing tool that you can utilize to achieve everything you desire. You'll discover that you'll literally create whatever you want in your life and you'll no longer be a victim of circumstances. Won't it be exciting to be the creator of the life you want to live? You can do it.

* * *

I believe that the reason so many people never achieve their goals is because they give up and fail to walk in that vibration we spoke about. The sad thing is that they have a choice. Bad things happen to all of us, but it is our choice to either tune into them or let them go with love and respect.

For example, you have started your day with short-term goals set in place and have great feelings attached to them when you leave your house. However, as you approach your office building you see that a terrible accident has just occurred. There are firetrucks, ambulances and medics and the scene is horrific. Of course, your first reaction will be one of shock. That's normal and empathetic. However, after that initial reaction, you now have a choice. You can embrace that fearful, horrified emotion and carry the feeling into your day, allowing it to influence your behavior. Many people would do so. They get so distracted with things going on around them and are easily pulled into negative feelings of fear and depression. That's when they lose the higher vibration and don't attract what they really want anymore – short- or long-term.

On the other hand, after seeing such a terrible accident you can walk into your building, say a prayer, wish the victims well, shake off the terrible images and carry on as planned. After all, there's nothing you can do about it. Isn't it so much more practical to tap back into the great feelings you had in the morning and allow them to help you achieve the goals you set in place for your day? It's up to you. You have the power.

* * *

When people think of goals, they often attached them to career, family or love life. Of course, that's important. However, for me a goal is not necessarily achieving the next step in a career or partnership. It involves so much more. For me it's really about what my soul wants to share with the world and what the next step in my life's journey will be. However, we're so programmed to focus on career and social status that we often set goals for things that are wrong for us and then become disappointed even when we achieve them. Remember what people say: Be careful what you wish for!

How many times have you had a secret desire but said to yourself, "You can't do this – you must work toward a more substantial career, must generate more income and must buy that expensive car!" There are so many musts that we lose sight of that for which our soul is longing.

I urge these folks to put that kind of thinking aside and instead ponder on what their lives would look like if they had their true hearts' desires. Life is so magical, my friends, and we need to connect to that great source that is the universe. We all have duties, but we need to find a way to balance them with what our true, long-term desires are. It's imperative to have faith, courage and trust.

I'm talking about the excitement of the journey, meeting new people and doing something that's really great for your soul – not for your partner, not for your family, not for society – but for you and your journey. This puts you on a higher level and you'll possess another kind of energy to motivate you and you'll attract many more resources, as well. You can create something new and exciting every day instead of letting your mind, education or society say, "Oh no, do your job and save your money because that's what's important." Is it really?

The answer to that question for me is "No!" That's why I loved living in Berlin so much. There I knew lots of Russian people – from the cleaning lady to the Rubenstein family – that I believe had the right goals and knew how to live life to the fullest. When they go out of the house, even to the store to buy some milk, they dress like they're on their way to a wedding because they never know what will happen that day. They may never see tomorrow.

When you celebrate with them, you can't say that you need to leave early because you have to go to work the next day. With them you learn to celebrate like it's the last day of your life. They know from experience what it's like to lose all their money. They also know from experience that they're always able to build it up again. I was intrigued by this.

Of course, this is an extreme example. Nevertheless, I believe that we should all take a little bit of this way of looking at life and apply it to our own lives. Learn to live for now. There's nothing wrong with setting career goals, but it's the way you view them that counts. I live somewhere in the middle between the material world and the spiritual world. One of my goals is sharing how to create wealth, value and a meaningful material life with the whole being and soul in a spiritual philosophy. I also wish to teach others how to use this spiritual philosophy to achieve their goals easily without fighting with their lives.

So, when setting goals, you should always focus on the bigger picture. What do you want to achieve when you become a CEO? Do you really need the responsibility of having people look at you and acknowledge that you're the boss? Maybe you'll have more money, but what will you be doing with the money? Perhaps you'll finally be able to fly first-class, instead of coach. Is that truly a motivation, though?

Funny thing is, I for one feel isolated in first-class. I always have fun and meet more people in coach. I would be very bored in my own jet! I enjoy the airport experience, getting a magazine and a cup of coffee, fighting for my overhead bin space and asking someone to help me put my bag up there. It usually starts a nice conversation that often times lasts the whole flight.

I also like interacting with the flight attendants. I was once in a business class seat and realized at the end of the flight that I wasted so much money because for 5 hours I was sitting in the kitchen area and chatting with the flight attendants. They showed me photos of their children, I showed them a pic of my daughter. Their lives were so inspiring – where they fly, what their days, nights and weekends are like. I had so much fun with them.

Okay, maybe I went off on a bit of a tangent with my propensity for flying coach! The point is that one of my goals in life is to have more experiences like that. Even if I wanted to be the CEO of my own company, the bigger goal for me would be having the financial security to be able to travel and meet more interesting folks. We all need to see goals in a bigger perspective.

It's all a journey and it's so very big. Get the most out of it. Once I had big houses in my life. I was so busy decorating them and throwing parties that I didn't spend time alone to figure out if this was one of my goals. I remember during one of my garden parties, I was looking at my guests as they ate hors d'oeuvres and sipped wine and asked myself if that was what really made me happy. I was just standing there, observing everyone making small talk with each other. Then I looked at myself making a show in my fabulous villa. But for what?

When I realized none of this was my goal, I changed my life and lived out of two suitcases for years. I was the happiest woman ever. I gave everything away and realized that I wanted to travel light. I like to rent now and don't get too attached to a property or anything material. Of course, I wouldn't travel to India with a backpack. My finances and life are secure. I'm just more aware and really observe myself when I set goals now.

SET GOALS

The fact is, I'm always setting new goals. We all need them. Think about what you really want and communicate with your partner. Put some time and thought into what really makes you happy. Maybe you can't afford 2 weeks in Thailand, but you can have a Thai massage or go to a Thai restaurant. I really miss being in Asia and communicating with those lovely people. So, when I'm in New York, I go to Chinatown. They have the fresh fish and vegetables out in the stands and I'm hearing Mandarin (I understand some of it) and it's all bringing me back to many happy times in Asia. They even have the best feet reflexology in Chinatown. You can only get it better in Asia. The sights, aromas and flavors are all so awesome. It's not fancy, but for me it's heaven on earth. This is what my goals are like. To have experiences like this that make me happy, because after all, that's what it's really about. Feeling happy.

* * *

I talked about a vision board before, but it's worth repeating here. When I set a new goal or want to achieve something special, I create a new vision board (I've had many!). Here's how you can make one for yourself. First, formulate a list of what you want to achieve and search for images which trigger a particular emotion in you, just as we talked about.

Then print out the images and pin or glue them to a canvas. I keep the canvas where I'll see it often, mostly near my desk. I also take a photo of it and save it on my cellphone and laptop so I can look at it when I'm not home. This keeps the emotions alive and is a tool that has helped me to pick up and move to different countries all over the world, ignoring everything that said I shouldn't! It's assisted me in achieving business goals as well and has attracted quality, loving people to my life. I'm so grateful for that.

* * *

Do you want to attain something special? You are in charge, so go for it. Don't let people or circumstances distract you because you are stronger than they are. Ignore them and stay the course. Keep focused on your goal, believe in it and know you are capable of achieving it yourself. The universe has your back and you can accomplish everything your beautiful soul desires. You have the tools so get started and set yourself free. This will be the first day of your new life!

MAKE A PLAN

AFTER YOU'VE ASCERTAINED WHAT YOU TRULY WANT – personal or professional – and have mindfully set your goals in place, you've taken the first important first step. Now you need a strategic plan to make it all happen. I always recommend starting with baby steps and scheduling them in your calendar so that you can actually see yourself approaching your dream step by step. After achieving a goal, I love to go back to the calendar and relive the journey in my mind.

We talked before about sending our dreams and desires out to the universe and waiting for an answer to arrive. We should all be doing this. However, some people then just sit back while they're waiting. Just waiting, without doing anything, is unreasonable behavior and it won't help you to realize your dreams. If you find yourself waiting for something too long and even worse, not moving to make it happen, don't worry. We'll talk about practical ways to avoid this and reset those habits in the next couple of chapters. Just be aware for now that the key here is to keep moving and putting yourself out there so that the right decisions and inspirations will come to you and move you closer to your goals. You can fast-track this if you have your plan in place, so that your actions are organized.

Sometimes there's a bit of trepidation attached to the whole process, especially if goals seem unattainable at first. That's just your mind kicking in with the analytics again. It tells you, "Oh no, you can't do this – it's impossible." So many people have a concept but they stop before they even start because practical thinking gets in the way. Be clever and outsmart your mind. If it helps, talk to it and say, "Hey, I heard this nonsense before but I know I have more potential than you're giving me credit for and I'm going to use my gifts to make this happen."

The truth is planning makes great things possible for everyone. You just need to start. I believe that the very first step in the planning process is to make a list. When I was moving to London from Bali, the task seemed daunting at first. I ignored the initial apprehensions and began my list. I needed an apartment and to set up my banking. I knew I required sheets, pillows, a coffee maker, etc. Then I researched the shops I would frequent. I would also need a cleaning lady. I wrote it all down and went back to it frequently to add or change items. The fear stopped because I knew I was taking my first baby steps toward bringing the project to its full manifestation.

For example, if your goal is to get a better job in a different industry, here's what your list might look like.

1. Find out what apps are the best to search for job offers.

2. When you note the qualifications of the job, research them to be sure you understand what they fully entail.

3. See if there's something you need to learn to be a proper candidate.

4. If so, then search for schools or online courses that will help you learn the skills you need.

5. Plan out how you can make the time required to integrate this course of study into your lifestyle.

6. If you need financial aid, check out the resources available to you.

7. If you don't qualify, think about someone from whom you can borrow the money.

8. If you can't find someone to lend you the money, take a look at your income and expenses. Perhaps you can quit the gym, download a yoga app, buy a mat and exercise at home. Or maybe you can incorporate daily runs into your schedule. These activities are all free of charge and will help you stay fit.

9. Set a time frame for yourself. It can include things like when you'll be finishing your studies, when you have to pay back a loan and when the best time to apply for the job would be.

10. Think about what else you can do to bring you closer to obtaining this job. How can you improve your networking skills and begin to

meet professionals in the new industry? This might lead to a fantastic recommendation.

11. Research how to create a resume that would suit the job application. Also look for examples of cover letters you can use as templates.

12. Investigate interviewing techniques and dress etiquette.

13. When you possess the qualifications you need for the job, send out your resume.

14. When you have found the right job and have been accepted, take it and start your new career.

15. Begin setting new goals.

This example of a list demonstrates that the desire to reach a goal is not enough to get what we want and have it be manifested in our lives. We need to start thinking practically and realistically, and there's nothing like a solid plan to make that happen. Of course, miracles always happen. If you put out to the universe that you needed to get out of debt and the next day you won a lottery, I wouldn't be surprised. The universe can work that way. However, we can't count on things like that. It's always more advisable, professional and practical to put your well thought out plan in place and begin your journey. Remember to be creative. Talk with people about your goals and you'll find that so many are willing to help and support you. It will all work out magically. That's a miracle in and of itself!

* * *

One of the by-products of learning to put plans in place to realize goals is that is trains you on how to be a leader, because that's exactly what leaders do. You'll be taking absolute responsibility for your life and your actions and you'll be in charge of your destiny. You'll keep moving every day and not only achieve your goal, but become more confident. Your self-image will also change and you'll have more respect for yourself because you'll be aware of your new inner strength and commitment. This charisma will be visible on the outside as well, and your energy and body language will attract more people like you into your life. It will also be a magnet for better circumstance to present themselves.

I guarantee, you'll set your sights on that $500,000 a year position you've been eyeing and won't wait for the company to send you an email asking if you'd consider taking the job. You'll know that's unrealistic. Instead, you'll count on yourself to make a plan and get started on your steps toward landing the job. And you will!

Of course, as you progress on your journey things will change and you might have to take a few detours and adapt a bit. So, it's best not to expect the steps in your plan to be written in stone. You shouldn't even envision the final manifestation of your desire or goal in specific terms. Be flexible with your plan.

You might, for instance, need to sacrifice something really important to you. That's part of the game and you'll discover that your desire to achieve your goal is stronger than the sacrifices you'll need to make. It won't be a big deal and I bet it won't even matter to you. The fact that you are indeed on the journey is all that will count. Moreover, what you'll learn from the journey will be invaluable to you. You will grow, you will create, you will discover.

Just keep moving, trust and believe in yourself and your plan and of course, never, ever give up. That's the way to make your goals happen and this is how you'll get there. How empowering is that?

13

DON'T WAIT

I'M NOT EXACTLY SURE WHY WE HUMAN beings often feel that we must wait before taking action. Perhaps at the source lies an underlying compulsion to hold back. If so, then I think it's more of an excuse not to act than a cautious hesitation – an insecurity about asserting ourselves. One thing is for certain, we do it all of the time.

Take emails, for example. There seems to be this unwritten rule that when you send an email, you need to give the person to whom it's addressed 24 hours to reply. If you don't get an answer within that time frame, what's your next move? Do you give the person another 24 hours? There's no guideline, but I'll bet you've been in this situation before and have felt that you'd be pushy or rude to send another email before a few days passed. So, you wait.

We feel that we need to give people their space, but what about our needs? There must be a middle ground between allowing someone respectable time to act and not allowing ourselves to be totally taken advantage of. I believe that we all need to be on top of situations like this. There's really no excuse for someone to not respond fairly quickly to an email – especially a pressing one – save a tragedy or illness. I have learned to respectfully expect (even, dare I say, demand) a quick reply.

Believe me, with my conservative background, it took me years to put this into practice. I was taught that I needed to show the utmost respect and be patient with people. That is, until I realized that when you wait for people you make their problems and hang-ups your own. Therefore, if you have an urgent – or even not so urgent – matter at hand and someone doesn't get back to you quickly, don't wait. Write again soon and say something like, "I'm sorry, did you get the message I sent you? I need to hear from you by the end of day because I have to make a decision." There's nothing wrong with that. You need to communicate quickly because you're responsible for yourself and your obligations and duties. If you don't receive a hasty reply, then quickly move on to the next option.

You might feel that this is hasty behavior or is even unfair to the person. Or perhaps you think that it's judgmental. As I said, if there are dire circumstances that can't be helped, of course you'll understand that. However, I think you'll find that in most cases it's just the person's M.O.

Moreover, it's been my experience that people don't change. So, don't wait and hope that he or she will turn over a new leaf. It's highly improbable. You'll always be chasing this person for answers and information that you need and you'll always be waiting far too long for them. That will only drain your energy and the only person that will be at a disadvantage is you. I therefore recommend that you stop dealing with that person completely, if you can manage it. Instead, surround yourself with reliable people who are on top of things. They'll always get back to you in time. If you continue to wait for people who aren't responsive, you'll only be setting yourself back.

In my experience, the absence of clear communication can cause a lack of a quick and timely responses. I've been in situations where I would hire a company to help me on a project, but they failed to say from the start that their organization grew too fast and didn't have enough employees to handle the job. Why didn't they communicate that in the beginning? They obviously didn't want to lose the opportunity and burdened their employees with more than they could handle.

So, I'd be waiting and waiting, wondering why these guys weren't getting back to me and meeting my deadlines. Of course, I found myself running after them and wasting time – and money. I finally resolved the problem by graciously telling them that I needed someone faster. They tried to convince me that they'd remedy the problem, but as I said, people don't change. So, I cut my losses and moved on. It takes courage at first, but you'll become accustomed to being responsible, taking care of yourself and demanding that people communicate clearly. You'll also learn to hone your vetting processes so that you'll avoid these situations in the future.

The speed and momentum in our Western culture is such that everything moves extremely fast. Time has therefore become more precious and valuable. In just a fraction of a second, we can send an email to someone across the globe or call them at no cost using WhatsApp. Therefore, when you wait, no matter what the situation, you lose. Someone else will jump on the job faster than you and you might very well miss an important opportunity. After all, all is fair in love, war...and business!

* * *

The previous examples speak to business situations. However, the same theory applies to your personal life. I found that so many people in my life had problems making decisions and that was often at the root of their inability to act. I just don't wait anymore.

Are you in a problematic situation with a family member or friend? Have you tried to call or text the person to no avail? How long will you wait for a response? Moreover, why should you even have to wait to get the problem resolved? That's unfair to you and will only negatively influence your emotions and damage your health because of the stress it's causing.

Moreover, if you wait too long, circumstances might change for the worse. It would be much better to take charge, take action and begin to resolve the problem yourself. When things are in motion and the person sees what's happening, I'll bet he or she calls you quickly to find out what's going on.

Perhaps this is your cue to take stock of your personal life and observe the people who surround you. How do they treat you? Are they always running late and making you wait for them? If so, they don't respect you or your valuable time. You need to make it clear that this is unacceptable behavior. Ask for the respect you deserve.

Also take note of people that only call when they need a favor. Ask yourself how many times they call just to ask how you are? Be aware of how you feel when you're with them. Are you inspired, energized and happy or irritated, tired and discontented to be with them? If you're feeling the latter, then make a change. Don't allow these people to pull you down with their negative auras. They'll never change, so just walk away and leave them behind. It's not harsh, it's self-preservation.

* * *

Incorporating a "Don't Wait" philosophy into your lifestyle doesn't only apply to problems. Let's say want to get away for the weekend and reach out to a friend to see if she'd like to join you. Your friend, however, just isn't responding and the weekend is drawing near. Perhaps you'd feel that because you already invited her, you can't change the agenda and therefore need to cancel your plans altogether. I say don't do that. Leave a message saying, "Hey, I haven't heard back so I'm going ahead and booking a hotel room now. If you can't get away, let me know. If I don't hear from you, have a great weekend." Then book your room and perhaps invite another friend. Or go yourself. I would, because I'm my best girlfriend anyway!

I've also discovered that doctor's offices are notorious for not getting back to you. If you've taken a test and the doctor was supposed to give you the results by Friday but doesn't call, then contact him and demand the results. Why should your weekend be ruined by worrying that something is wrong? You should also consider changing doctors. Remember, you and you alone are responsible for your health and emotional state-of-being.

* * *

You've heard it before, but it bears repeating: "Tell me whom you're with and I'll tell you who you are?" There's a lot of truth to that statement. That's why you should devote a good deal of energy choosing the people you'll spend time with in your personal and business life. Go with the leaders who inspire, motivate and support you.

I personally have realized that after many years of trying, I'll just never get the respect I deserve from certain people in my life. This rings true especially with certain family members. When I try to communicate with them, if feels like I'm speaking German and they're speaking Chinese. We just don't connect. Moreover, we totally don't understand each other. It's just the way it is.

As I told you, for years I tried to be the family darling to everyone. That only resulted in my feeling empty, depressed and lonely – as if I had betrayed myself. Then I met a woman who was the same age as my mother, who had passed away when I was 29 years old. Her name was Renate, and she always told me, "Verena, those people are who they are and you are you." It was a simple message, but I took it to heart and realized that I couldn't walk away from certain family members, but I could set healthy boundaries with them and instead spend my time working on myself. I learned to respect myself more and didn't let people pull me down or waste my time. Renate taught me a valuable lesson.

You have the skills and authority to create awesome accomplishments in your life – whether they're personal or business goals. Surround yourself with quality people because they'll be the team players with whom you'll achieve remarkable successes. Remember, we chose the souls who are to walk on this journey with us. Embrace the power, take advantage of your connection with the universe and use your instincts to recognize these souls. Then just walk away from those with whom you were not meant to be. Don't let them hold you back by making you wait for them. Take back control, move on and tap into your strength and higher vibrations to reach your goals and create the life you want and deserve to live.

14

KEEP MOVING

EVERY TIME I DECIDED TO MOVE TO another country, I had to face many, many challenges. What exasperated these situations was that I always had a problem with authority – something that popped up when dealing with visas, legal documents, banks, etc. In addition, there was always a fear factor that I needed to address.

When I started to prepare for my move to London, I needed to open a bank account. Unfortunately, the banker I was dealing with was a very difficult person. In fact, he seemed to have issues with his job, which made things even worse. When I first spoke with him, he was cold and arrogant. He told me – in a very nasty way – that he wouldn't be able to open a bank account because there would be a post box number on my bank statement. I already knew that in some countries they don't deliver mail to your door. Instead, they leave you a note telling you to collect your mail at the post office. So, something wasn't jiving here.

He was very obstinate about the whole thing and it became readily apparent that this huge bank was not aware of the post box situation in some countries or they just simply weren't interested in working with international clients. My first reaction was to become very upset and nervous and my fear started to rear its ugly face. "Oh my God, Verena, you can't move to London without a bank account!" Then I calmed down and thought about the predicament. I remembered that I had done this before, and was able to provide the banker with a statement from another bank that had a post box address on it. When he saw that, he reconsidered and opened the account for me.

After an hour of paperwork, I had the account in place. He then asked me if I wanted to perform transactions online. I told him that I did require that. Unfortunately, he had a problem getting it to function because I had had an account with this bank before and the system wasn't allowing me to set up credentials for online access. The banker's bad attitude came to the surface once again and he began treating me like an idiot, saying, "What did you do? You must have set it up incorrectly."

That was my turning point. Although I would have loved to stop right there, tell him to cancel everything and report him to his superiors, I decided to keep moving and fight. After all, I required online banking and I already wasted enough time. The last thing I needed was to start the whole procedure all over again with another bank. I therefore told him in a very determined voice that I had set up the online banking correctly and that there had to be something wrong with their internal system. I insisted that he contact the Call Center and fix the problem immediately.

After 2 rigorous hours, it all worked out. The banker's demeanor changed dramatically and he respectfully asked me to contact the Call Center and tell them that I was satisfied with his service. I smiled and told him I would. It didn't matter to me because I had accomplished what I started out to do and was prepared to work on the next project for my move.

* * *

I'm convinced that when people don't reach their goals or see the manifestation of their dreams, it's because they've stopped moving. It seems most folks easily give up when something goes wrong and they hit obstacles in their journeys. I find this illogical. After all, if you're headed to Puerto Rico and sitting on a delayed plane, you wouldn't get off because the flight isn't departing on time? If you're sitting in a taxi and hit some traffic, would you ask the driver to turn around and take you back home? Of course not! You move on. This is precisely what you should do as you walk your journey toward your goals.

I think it's vital to always remember that commitment is important. We don't seem to have a problem keeping to a commitment when we have skin in the game. For instance, when we hit bumps in the road, we don't think of walking away from a financial investment. It's easier for people to keep moving in these circumstances.

However, when it's about a goal that we've set for ourselves – without financial investment – and we have a couple of bad days, negativity sets in. We need to remember at these times that when we start moving toward a goal, there will be unexpected potholes and detours because that's part of that journey. Instead, we let these events irritate us and cause us to become insecure. We start to ask ourselves, "Am I on the right road or did I make a bad decision?" We think too much and even long to move backward instead of forward, wanting to surround ourselves with old circumstance that were familiar in our comfort zone. We forget the commitment we made to the journey and then only focus on doubts, immediately giving up without a fight.

Don't allow your fears to pull you back and stop you from moving forward. Realize that it all ties into our insecurities, doubts and fears and that's normal. We're all human and believe me, it's much scarier to give up and stop moving than it is to stay the course. You'll come to know that with experience.

Our journeys are all filled with wonder and magic. The fact is anything can happen along the way and we really can't control it – but that's actually a gift! By facing new challenges and obstacles, we grow and learn new things. This enriches our skills and our souls. Just take it step by step and do the best you can. When obstacles appear, tap into your male energy. Be strong, be a warrior and fight for what you want. If something doesn't work this way, try another way. The change in course won't bother you because you'll start to see the new way as a process rather than a final state of being.

Think of it as planting a seed into the soil. You water it, care for it and wait. It will germinate and one day break through the surface of the ground, making itself known to the world. That's how you should view starting a new journey. Your goal will surface if you just keep nourishing it, no matter what happens along the way.

Of course, it's the unknown that scares us. Just be aware of it and know that since you've committed to the journey and the goal is important to you, you'll be more sensitive than usual. So, treat yourself gently and with patience. Also remember to love yourself for embarking on the journey and keep moving through the obstacles because they will pass.

*　*　*

We've talked about how important it is to "Keep Moving" when reaching for our goals. However, it applies to other circumstances in our lives. I think it would be great if everyone were to put a note on their bathroom mirror that says, "Keep Bicycling!" Maybe it should be accompanied by a photo of someone in a race! I say this because life is very much like a marathon.

I believe that change is one of the most difficult things people face in their lives – both personal and professional. Change is scary, for sure. The thing is that we need to alter the way we view it, as well as the manner in which we deal with it.

Our lives are based on a tripod of three legs: Family/Relationships, Career and Home. If you change one of these, your foundation becomes a bit unstable. If you change two, even more unsteady. If you change all three, you'll lose stability altogether and will have to start completely anew. I would never suggest changing each leg of your life all at once, but you should examine the amount of change you're making at any particular time in your life and use it as the barometer that measures your fears and insecurity.

How much are you planning to change in your life right now? Whatever your answer, expect that there will be anxiety and fright in the beginning but don't let that stop you short. Remember, embracing the fear as a sign that an opportunity is present is the way to go. Just keep moving because that's the only way to reach a goal and realize a new and exciting way of living your life. Honestly, it's quite simple yet still very difficult at times. Sometimes you'll feel overwhelmed and won't want to push yourself outside of your comfort zone. Just keep going and don't allow yourself to look right, left and never, ever backward. Just look forward.

If, for example, you're leaving an unhealthy relationship, don't think about the good times. Keep reminding yourself about the disappointments of the relationship. You can recall the good times later on when you're stronger and over the separation or divorce. At the moment, though, anything that's good for you can only lie ahead. You'll make it if you keep your body, mind and soul in motion, believe in yourself and trust in the process and the bigger plan. You'll develop like that seed in the soil. One day, very soon, you'll face the light and rise above the earth.

There are some fringe benefits to the process. You'll grow to be more confident and develop better behavioral skills to utilize in your next relationship, as well. You'll also learn to put your emotions aside, when necessary, and really start to act as the leader of your life and destiny, embracing the positive energy that the universe provides us all.

To "Keep Moving" also applies to everyday situations that aren't as monumental as a major change in one of the three legs of our lives. There are those day-to-day circumstances where we often find ourselves stuck and unable to decide. That's okay. Here's where we can repeat the exercise we've talked about before. Don't stop moving, just take the day off and don't think about it. If negative thoughts intrude, say "No!" to them and think about something totally different. As I've said before, use your power and potential by handing it over to your higher self and then ask for a roadmap, a solution. The universe will have received your request and placed your order. Keep moving by taking responsibility and trusting in the universe. Get up the next day and you'll see that solutions in the form of a call, email or article will be delivered as ordered. But you have to keep moving and act upon the message you've received. You need to be in the game, because a sure way to fail is to do nothing and drop out. When you move, you're a player and you're always on your feet!

* * *

I learned to "Keep Moving" fairly early in my life because I saw such great examples of it when I was very young. When I was 12 years old, my mother suffered from an immobilizing period of depression. She used to just sit on the sofa or at the table like a doll. My father hired a woman to bathe, clothe and feed her so she was always well taken care of, but she wasn't living. She was just existing, and barely at that.

It was like that for a year. In those days, no one was really talking about depression. It was misunderstood as insanity or just laziness. My father didn't give up on her, though. He kept moving and did the best he could to keep her sitting up. I guess he must have relied on his intuition because after a year she eventually came out of it. It was slow going in the beginning. First, she was encouraged to walk around the house. Then she began strolling in the garden. Step by step my father kept her moving. She kept – sometimes even forced – herself to move through it, too. The one thing I learned is to never keep someone who is depressed in bed. If you get them out of bed, they're already on their way to getting better and becoming heroes.

Speaking of heroes, I'd like to tell you about my grandmother. She lived alone for a very long time because she was widowed early in her marriage. Until the age of 96, she remained an elegant woman with long, grey hair that she fixed like Grace Kelly.

Grandma couldn't hear very well but refused hearing aids because they were made of plastic and she wanted to live totally naturally, without man-made materials. When she received a new hip, no one told her because if she knew her hip had artificial material in it, she's be mortified. They simply told her that the doctors fixed it in surgery naturally. She was quite a character!

I mention Grandma here because she is one of the finest examples of a person who always kept moving. She got out of bed every day, fixed her hair and dressed herself impeccably, even if she wasn't expecting visitors. She was also very organized. She asked my sister to bring her fresh eggs every Saturday at 3 pm. She would have everything ready for my sister's arrival, including tea and a snack, and then would sit close to where the bell was to ring so she could hear it. This was every Saturday, rain, shine or snow!

One Saturday, my sister came twenty minutes late. Growing impatient, Grandma moved away from the bell to do something, so when it rang she didn't hear it. My sister panicked and asked a couple who looked after Grandma to open the door. Grandma was so angry because she didn't want the couple to know she had problems hearing!

Grandma may have been a bit too proud, but she impressed me so because she always got out of bed, even though she was in her nineties, and made herself ready for the day ahead of her. I'm sure at her age she suffered pain from arthritis, but she didn't let that stop her. She was always dressed to the nines and never in a bathrobe. She got her chores done and kept moving.

Right before she died, we all spent Christmas together. Grandma seemed as normal as ever. In the beginning of January, though, she called my Dad, who was her only son and asked him to visit her. Dad didn't think much of it, until he arrived and found her lying in bed with a beautiful night jacket on, her hair in a net. He was shocked to see her that way, until she explained to him that she was ready to leave this world.

My father called his sisters and they all came to be with her and say goodbye. She lay in bed for 14 days with her family around her, and then she just fell asleep. She didn't stop moving, though. She just moved on.

* * *

I know you want to achieve something bigger in your life. By all means, fight for it! Some spiritual teachers say that when something comes easy, it's usually for a short-term experience. It will disappear as quickly as it arrived. Long-term experiences usually come with a more difficult price, but they're so worth it.

Every day and every step you take brings you closer and closer to your target. When reaching for a goal, don't think too much and don't analyze excessively. You'll be wasting valuable time and energy. Just keep moving forward.

Because you're the master of your life, you have choices. The universe gave you that authority. When you set your mind to making your dream happen, there's nothing that can hold you back. Trust and believe in the real power inside yourself. It's so much bigger than you could ever imagine.

HOW I FACED MY FEARS

Embrace it without drama or tears. When you keep moving, the world will take notice! More power to you!

15

BE THANKFUL

GRATITUDE IS A TOOL THAT HOLDS SO much power and energy in it. In fact, being thankful changes your attitude and vibration immediately. For me, it's one of the most important keys to being fulfilled and truly happy in my life.

You've no doubt heard the expression, "Count your blessings." Try this. Look around you – take as long as you need – and then list on a note pad how many things in your life for which you can be grateful. Notice how doing this exercise changes your perspective and the way you see your life. Instead of taking things for granted or even worse, looking at things negatively – both of which give us no pleasure at all – you suddenly find yourself rejoicing in the gifts the universe has given you. View your life this way and suddenly everything is filled with love. It lifts you and your spirit to another level of being.

Unfortunately, many people forget to be thankful. I'm not sure if they're ungrateful, but they certainly are complacent. They live in beautiful homes and drive expensive cars, but they're too busy focusing on what to buy next than being thankful for what they already have. These poor people are looking for immediate gratification in the form of material things or acknowledgement from other people. The real happiness, however, comes with living, breathing and loving in this life. I guess we all, at one time or another, forget this.

Even during the roughest of times, you'll always find things for which to be thankful. Life is your journey and its purpose is to create experiences, which allow you to grow, learn and develop yourself. Life is never black or white and everything has its own time. It's a complicated business, and when something ends it's best to just be thankful and let it go. Whatever it was, don't look at it judgmentally and don't doubt yourself. It's up to you to see what valuable lessons you've learned and then be thankful and move on.

* * *

When you examine your life with grateful eyes, at first you'll tend to list the major components of your existence, such as health, wealth, family and loving relationships. I always ask people to then continue the exercise on a daily basis, and take note of everything that you experience, no matter how small. When you do this, you'll find yourself saying "Thank You!" to the universe all day long.

When I stay at my daughter's apartment in New York City, I never take the visit for granted. I can't help but think how wonderful and amazing it is to be in this vibrant city in such a beautiful apartment. It's such a gift, honor and pleasure and I'm so grateful for it.

I have my daily routine during my stay. While my daughter is at work, there's this small place I frequent to pick up lunch every day. They've gotten to know me and now I'm part of the family there. We talk about how the day is going and have a good time chatting with each other. It's just for a few minutes, but I go home with my delicious salad and am so thankful for this daily experience. It's so joyful.

During the evenings I often get into an Uber car that's clean and when the driver brings me to my destination in comfort, I think, "What an honor!" I sit in one of the city's many lovely restaurants and a wonderful server brings me such delicious food. Once again I say to myself, "This is heaven on earth!" I'm so thankful that I'm there to see, smell and taste the experiences. On the way home, I might stroll Fifth Avenue and window shop the elegant stores. I don't have to buy anything to think, "How lucky am I to experience this day?"

During one of my visits to New York City, I was having a problem with my debit card and needed to go to the main branch of the bank. I was hot, tired and hungry and not feeling very well until I was greeted by this very nice, young man. It took us an hour to solve the problem, but I have to say he was so pleasant and professional that I didn't mind. By the end of our time together, I was sitting in his chair, looking at his computer. We talked about our lives and he told me he planned to check out my website. Now feeling refreshed, I walked home in the sunlight, the weather a bit cooler at that hour, and realized that what began as a stressful day ended so nicely. I was so thankful for this experience.

It's all about seeing the joy in the little things as well as the big and being thankful for all of it because this gratitude gives us so much joy. I find such amazement in a cup of coffee with a friend, the smell of a gardenia or a warm, summer breeze. When you experience things such as these throughout your day, give thanks and you'll enjoy them all the more.

We've talked about this before but it bears repeating: Don't allow yourself to get lost and bogged down with worrying. Stop talking, stop thinking, stop analyzing. Be in the here and now. I saw a man walking into my daughter's building lobby talking to someone on his cell phone. While doing that he addressed himself to the doorman, then began speaking once again to the person on the phone, and went back and forth like this for 10 minutes. He was so oblivious and I thought, "Hey, we're on planet earth here! Where are you?" It's amazing how many people are just not present. I feel sorry for them. We all need to be in the moment – take time to smell the roses, as they say. We travel too quickly and the transition from points A to B is being lost. We're just not enjoying each moment. You need to be aware to be thankful, and you can find gratitude in the smallest things. All you have to do is open your eyes. It lifts you and gives you a super benefit because you'll feel rich in terms of happiness and warmth and you'll attract more and more happy experiences.

* * *

Sometimes gratitude comes right away, especially when you're used to looking at your life that way. Other times, though, it comes from experiences that are at first disappointing. A good example of this was my time in Bali, where I lived for one-and-a-half years. Although it was the most exotic place I ever called home, after a while I realized that it didn't suit me. It was far too small for what I wanted to achieve in my life.

At first, I was disappointed in myself for moving there. I kept wondering why I decided to relocated to Indonesia in the first place. How could I have made such a mistake? While on a trip to London, which was to be my next city of residence, I began to understand why I had chosen Bali in the first place. I had been tired of juggling a career and being a single mother in a fast-moving society. I longed for an easy-paced, warmer place to live. Bali gave me time to slow down and reexamine my life. It was kind of a pit-stop, if you will.

It was in Bali that I realized what I needed. After my daughter started living her own life in New York City, I wanted to begin a new chapter for myself and once again live among diverse people in a vibrant city. Although I had lived in a bustling city before, this time I was ready to draw energy and excitement from the frenetic atmosphere – to be a part of that society and lifestyle.

After reflecting alone for a while, I also understood that when I moved to Bali I was emotionally exhausted and very disappointed in my circumstances at that time. Bali really healed me. The way the Balinese see the world and how they live their lives in itself is restorative and curing. Their easier lifestyle is achieved by strictly following the rules of Hinduism. They talk to each other all the time and this constant communication allows them to know what each person must do. It's a community where everyone supports each other – living, working and praying together. It's such a contrast to our Western culture and it taught me so many valuable lessons in the short time I lived there.

I am now so grateful for the time I spent in Bali. It rejuvenated me and gave me what I needed to once again live with technology, which allows us all to be free and heightens creativity and energy. Of course, that always goes hand-in-hand with being responsible for myself and my needs. I was ready for the challenge. Thank you, Bali!

* * *

Like so many gifts of the universe, being thankful is a magical experience. When you're aware of your emotions, surroundings and wishes and view what's going on in your life through grateful eyes, you open doors to even more exciting possibilities and experiences.

See the world as an innocent child does. Choose wonder over anger or judgement and observe what a positive impact it has on you. Yes, being thankful opens up the doors to a higher level of living filled with more meaning and value. It will also attract people and circumstances into your life which have similar intentions and vibrations.

Always being thankful can also help you deal with difficult people. For example, if you are irritated or angry with someone, the first thing you should ask is, "Was he motivated to hurt me or just unaware of what he was doing?" If you find that there really was no motivation, calm down and open yourself up to seeing the situation as a means to better communication with the person and then be grateful for the opportunity. In most cases, the situation is not as problematic as you think. You're able to solve it without judging and you'll benefit from your open-mindedness. Now you can be thankful that you created a positive experience and grew from it. Isn't that wonderful?

How you act defines you and how you see the world affects how others view you. If you express your thoughts in a more thankful way, it will influence your actions, emotions, charisma and health. You have that power to decide how you want to act in this world. Gratitude for what you have brings even more of what you want into your life and raises your state of being, your relationships and endless possibilities.

Indeed, gratitude is a decision. Use this tool to raise yourself. It will bring so much joy and, after all, you deserve it.

16

HAVE RESPECT

I THINK THAT RESPECT LIVES ON THE opposing side of ego. That's why some people feel that if they show respect to another person they somehow diminish themselves, which of course is not true.

I find it sad that we are the only species on the planet that hurt each other consciously. You just don't see that in nature. Of course, when animals are hungry they kill but that's survival and actually serves an ecological purpose in the grand order of things. This differs vastly from human behavior, which often involves fighting and hurting each other for no critical reason.

When I say human beings, I actually don't mean to imply the entire species. For instance, with just a few exceptions, I found the opposite to be true in Bali. During my time there, I grew to know and love many Balinese friends and observed them and their customs closely. They're big on weekly rituals and come together during these ceremonies as one. I usually attended with my business partner and learned so much from Balinese gatherings.

Everyone at the meetings knows where everyone else comes from and what level of ranking they hold in their society. The higher-ranking people are usually those who are educated, own businesses and have some wealth. The lower ranks usually include manual laborers, housekeepers, etc. The thing that is most fascinating is that societal status doesn't matter to these people at all. The moment they enter the room they begin mingling and talking with each other without judgement, even though they're fully aware of the different economic and social levels they occupy. The cleaning lady and the business person sit next to each other, smile and treat each other with mutual respect.

It was also astonishing to me that in Bali no one puts a price on any service. They always leave it up to you to decide what you'd like to pay them. Because there's always present a mutual respect and trust for each other, they know that the pricing will always be fair. They also believe in helping each other out and if they can afford it, they'll be generous.

I discovered this when I hired my cleaning lady. She wouldn't give me an hourly rate and insisted that I determine what her work was worth to me. We agreed on a price and, to be honest, because she asked me to decide I probably gave her more than she would have ask for. Nevertheless, I was happy with our arrangement and very satisfied with her work. In fact, when I knew there was to be a really big ceremony approaching, I would give her more that week to help her pay for what she and her family needed to participate. I respected her and it made me happy. All I asked was that she pray for me at the ceremony.

* * *

HAVE RESPECT

Life would be so much better on the whole if people would just learn respect others more. That respect is almost always returned and it becomes another thankful experience to enjoy. At the very least, we should all respect each other for just being human because that is the one thing that we all have in common.

Respect would come easily if people learned to be more open and communicate with each other. Instead, we seem to be programmed to judge one another. This one is uneducated, the other is gay and that one there is way too nosey. This leads to disrespect which is ridiculous because, for goodness sake, we were all human beings before we became anything else! We came into this world the same way, we all breathe in and out to stay alive and we all put on our shoes in the morning before walking out of the house. Don't these common bonds deserve mutual respect? It doesn't always seem to be so, though.

We need to find a balance between enforcing ourselves and our needs and really connecting honesty with each other. This, for some, becomes a challenge when dealing with those who work for them or are serving them in one capacity or the other. They tend to conduct themselves in a more distant manner – even behaving a bit arrogantly – because they think they must adhere to some sort of social order. Or it may very well stem from an insecurity about their own self-worth and they feel that disrespecting people will somehow elevate their own status.

I observe this tendency when I visit the nail salon for a pedicure and manicure. I really dislike the way certain customers treat the technicians like servants. They never say "Please" and they never utter the words "Thank You." Don't they realize what a gift these wonderful women are giving their feet and hands? I've become friends with manicurists and pedicurists and view them as "nail specialists," women whom I respect and to whom I am extremely grateful.

I have learned to do this everywhere a service is provided. In restaurants, I consider servers in very high regard. It's indeed a difficult job and think of what a gracious gift they give us as they serve us delicious food and ask us if we need anything to make our visit there more enjoyable. I always make eye contact with them and say "Thank You!" I will even go as far to say that I consider them angels when they pour me another glass of wine! I mean, how lovely is that?

When traveling, I always smile at people and even make an attempt to speak with them. Whether it's someone cleaning the restrooms in the airport or the hotel porter, I greet them, ask how they're doing that day and thank them for their service. If I encounter them again, they remember me and take the time to ask how my day is going. They treat me like a princess! It touches my heart that such small gestures can have such a huge impact on our lives.

When you show respect with an open heart, you'll always receive it a hundredfold. Here's a good example. I used to travel to Singapore regularly for business, so I always tried to book a nice hotel to enjoy my stay as much as possible. At the Fullerton Hotel I became very friendly with the porters who worked there. I liked them very much and considered them heroes because they had to wear heavy uniforms in the intense heat but never complained. The level of service was astounding and they were such amiable men.

One day I took my place on the taxi line in front of the hotel. There were a few women standing in front of me who were looking at me in what seemed a very judgmental way. Perhaps, in this very traditional society, they felt I wasn't

HAVE RESPECT

dressed conservatively enough. Or maybe they just didn't appreciate the fact that I was European and different from them. In any event, they weren't being very friendly.

One of the older porters I knew well saw this so he approached me, took my arm and led me to a taxi even though I was standing at the back of the line. Well, you should have seen the looks on those women's faces. It was a combination of shock and anger! The porter and I had a chat and laughed about it. I told him that he made me feel like a celebrity and in fact, made my day.

It's important to remember that people who work in service industries such as hotels, restaurants, salons and airlines are at the heart of the business. We very seldomly get to talk to the CEO of these companies. If we did, it really wouldn't get us better service anyway because they're way too disconnected with the everyday happenings of the business. No, our experiences are always dependent upon the folks who serve the customers directly. These are the ones with whom we connect and communicate. When you treat them warm-heartedly and respectfully you receive a lot of support from them and therefore will enjoy an encounter that you'll never forget.

It's even more than being nice as a means to receiving good service. You need to respect these people because they are fellow human beings and it's the right thing to do. Don't get hung up on the fact that you're the customer – the boss – and that makes you right no matter what. When you think "This person is here to serve me and the customer is always right" you're setting yourself up for an unhappy experience. Instead, show respect and gratitude. Not only will you get better service, you'll be happier for it.

* * *

It's important to note that in general, there is a lack of respect in our society and it has become a grave problem. This applies to a lack of respect for animals, as well. Just watch any ASPCA commercial and you'll be devastated at how dogs and cats are being treated. It's unacceptable. Animals raised for slaughter in the U.S. are often horribly mistreated as well.

It's no better in Korea and Indonesia, where they eat dogs. That's part of their culture, but it's the way they treat and kill the dogs that is so abominable. Add to that what happens on safaris in Africa, and it becomes abundantly clear that a lack of respect for everything has become somewhat the norm in our society.

We need to start respecting animals, the earth and of course, each other – regardless of nationality, color, race, creed or economic position.

* * *

Treating other people with respect shows that you respect yourself as well. So, in a sense self-respect is at the foundation of how you treat others. How do you know if you truly have respect for who you are? Ask, "How do I treat myself?" Do you feel love and compassion or when you look in the mirror do you experience feelings of self-deprivation or denial?

It's more than looking into a mirror, though. That's a good start, but you really need to take a deeper look within. What are your inner conversations like? Do you ask yourself "Why am I such an idiot?" when you react to a situation badly?

Or when a plan goes sideways, do you comfort yourself by saying "It doesn't matter because I did my very best"? If the latter is true, then you're treating yourself with love and are connected to your inner child. You possess a gift because you're friends with yourself and are committed to that friendship. This will all reveal itself in your outside behavior with other people. You'll respect them naturally.

We're all connected and people will sense internally how you feel about them. They might not be consciously aware of it, but they'll feel it nonetheless. That makes life and interactions with people so fascinating. It doesn't even require words in many cases. So, if you walk with respect at your core, you don't need to go out of your way to show people you like them. Just like and respect them and they'll feel it. Then watch how amazing possibilities will follow.

On the other hand, if you really don't like someone, you also don't need to say anything because they'll feel that as well. However, there's no need to treat them with disrespect. Remember the rule of Karma, "What goes around, comes around." Just keep your distance because you weren't meant to walk your journey with them anyway. The universe is telling you that.

Decide to work or play with people you like and mutual respect will follow. Without it, peaceful coexistence and interactions will be impossible to achieve. It's really a simple rule to follow – every relationship in your life depends on respect to work.

At the end of the day, we're all just trying to walk the paths of our journeys with dreams, desires and sometimes doubts. When others' paths run parallel to yours, strive for teamwork and you'll feel connected to them. That's a wonderful thing because you don't have to walk the journey all by yourself. When you seem to be losing respect because of insecurity or misunderstandings, put your ego on a shelf and step over that obstacle. It's so worth it because you'll feel elevated and energized as you connect with a higher vibration.

Sometimes people don't make it easy for us. I know. However, when this happens strive to push your emotions aside, work together and the solutions will emerge. This will really help you reach your goals. You'll also have an emotional advantage because it will enable you to enjoy your journey in harmony and good health. You'll feel fulfilled and your life will be so much more joyous. That's the ultimate goal for us all!

www.ingramcontent.com/pod-product-compliance
Lightning Source LLC
LaVergne TN
LVHW051523070426
835507LV00023B/3278